Maths Investigations

A Collection of Open-ended Tasks

How long would it take to write every number to a million?

Why is my birthday on a different day each year?

How many nappies will a baby use before he or she is toilet-trained?

Can a person really jump from the top of one building to the next like they do on TV?

Is it true that the length of your foot is the same as the distance between your elbow and your wrist?

How much water do I use having a shower?

Published by Prim-Ed Publishing

Written by Paul Swan

0094–UK

FOREWORD

The National Numeracy Strategy states that providing children with non-routine problems, which require them to think for themselves, is a factor that promotes high standards of numeracy.

So often the mathematics we present to children has been sanitised to the point where all they need to do is follow a few remembered procedures in order to answer straightforward questions. Unfortunately, most questions we face in life are never straightforward and we need to apply our problem-solving skills in order to arrive at an answer—or one of a number of possible answers. Seldom do the problems we encounter contain all the information we require and so we need to seek out further information. At other times we are faced with problems that contain too much information and we must determine what information is relevant and what is not.

This book is designed around a set of open-ended questions, many of which are drawn from magazines, newspapers and life experiences. As such many of the questions are 'messy' and involve sifting through information and collecting further information. To assist teachers, detailed notes providing extra hints and information have been provided. It is recommended, however, that teachers use discretion as to how and when this extra information is used. Let the children ask questions and seek out information before telling them too much. When they arrive at a solution or a possible set of solutions, then encourage them to discuss the range of answers or the reasons for settling on a single answer. As children become experienced working with open questions you will find that they discover more questions that require answers and so it goes on.

Many thanks to Geoff White for his inspiration.

CONTENTS

Teachers Notes	ii	Typing a Million	40 – 41
Curriculum Links	iii	A Feel for Big Numbers	42 – 43
8 000 Nappies	2 – 3	A Million Dots	44 – 45
The Pencil Case Problem 1	4 – 5	List of Large Numbers	46 – 47
The Pencil Case Problem 2	6 – 7	Metric Paper 1	48 – 49
Tape Measure	8 – 9	Metric Paper 2	50 – 51
Take a Flying Leap	10 – 11	Paper, Paper Everywhere	52 – 53
Big Foot	12 – 13	My Legs Hurt	54 – 55
Down the Drain	14 – 15	Popcorn Packets	56 – 57
Pieces of Eight	16 – 17	Measure Matters 1	58 – 59
The Money Trail	18 – 19	Measure Matters 2	60 – 61
Competition Maths	20 – 21	Measure Matters 3	62 – 63
Crossing the Road	22 – 23	Measure Matters 4	64 – 65
Tinkering with Time	24 – 25	Coin Capers	66 – 67
Metric Time	26 – 27	The Largest Organ in Your Body	68 – 69
Calendar Corrections	28 – 29	The Language of Maths	70 – 71
The World Calendar	30 – 31	Projections, Enlargements and Distortions	72 – 77
The Calendar	32 – 33	Who Rubbed the Blackboard?	78 – 79
Four Calendars	34 – 35	The Broken Calculator	80 – 81
Calendar Conundrums	36 – 37	Where to Go from Here	83
Writing a Million	38 – 39		

Teachers Notes

This publication is designed around a set of stimulus sheets designed to set children:

- thinking
- talking, and
- researching

to solve a problem.

Leading mathematics educator Paul Trafton believes that teachers should '… make maths messy …' in order to encourage children to think in mathematics. When you consider it, most mathematics in real life is messy. Either you don't possess enough information to solve the problem and you have to search for more or you are given too much information and you need to discard some. Often in real life there is no one right answer but a variety of answers each equally valid depending upon the circumstances at the time. To illustrate, consider all the different mobile phone plans available—trying to compare and choose the best one is rather complicated.

The availability of technology such as calculators, computers and the Internet have now made it possible to ask open-ended questions within a classroom setting. Children working on open-ended investigations will often need to use calculators because the numbers will come from real data. They will also need to ask clarifying questions, make assumptions, estimate, survey, locate information and generally follow the pattern that people do when solving open-ended questions.

As a teacher, I would encourage you to have fun messing about with the children or the questions. This will require a level of risk-taking but a wealth of support material has been provided to compliment each stimulus sheet. The support material often provides the data required to 'solve' the problem or ideas for extending the problem or simply background information and stories to help the problem live in the minds and hearts of the children. Where possible, historical and cultural links to the mathematics contained on the stimulus page have been provided so that a context for the problem may be given.

A word of caution—to gain the most from these open-ended investigations, children will need to be given the time to:

- discuss the problem;
- ask questions;
- explore the problem;
- ask questions; and
- explain the problem (present their findings).

Expect children, in fact encourage them, to explore various aspects of the problem; some will even go off at a tangent to the problem (that is how you will find new mathematics to explore). Fire their imagination, learn along with them and boldly go where few have been before.

Curriculum Links

Maths Investigations contains a collection of open-ended tasks covering many of the objectives from the Numbers and the Number System, Calculations, Measures, Shape, Space and Handling Data strands of the Numeracy Strategy. Completion of these activities will provide opportunities for children to cover the following objectives from the Solving Problems strand of the Numeracy Strategy.

Year	Strand	Content Objectives
4	Solving problems	• choose and use appropriate number operations and appropriate ways of calculating to solve problems • explain methods and reasoning about numbers • solve mathematical problems or puzzles, recognise and explain patterns and relationships, generalise and predict • suggest extensions by asking 'What if....?' • make and investigate a general statement about familiar numbers or shapes • use all four operations to solve word problems involving numbers in 'real life', money and measures, using one or more steps
5	Solving problems	• choose and use appropriate number operations and appropriate ways of calculating to solve problems • explain methods and reasoning, orally and in writing • solve mathematical problems or puzzles, recognise and explain patterns and relationships, generalise and predict • suggest extensions by asking 'What if....?' • make and investigate a general statement about familiar numbers or shapes • use all four operations to solve word problems involving numbers and quantities based on 'real life', money and measures, using one or more steps
6	Solving problems	• choose and use appropriate number operations and appropriate ways of calculating to solve problems • explain methods and reasoning, orally and in writing • solve mathematical problems or puzzles, recognise and explain patterns and relationships, generalise and predict • suggest extensions by asking 'What if....?' • make and investigate a general statement about familiar numbers or shapes • identify and use appropriate operations (including combinations of operations) to solve word problems involving numbers and quantities based on 'real life', money or measures, using one or more steps

TEACHER BACKGROUND

8 000 NAPPIES

As a father of twins in nappies, this article in Choice magazine—the official journal of the Australian Consumers' Association—caught my eye. (www.choice.com.au)

The question offers many opportunities for investigation beyond the collection of data. For example, consider the environmental impact of 8 000 disposable nappies multiplied by the number of children wearing nappies in a particular country.

This question allows students the opportunity to collect primary data. There are always pregnant mums or mums with young children in and around primary schools. Pupils could design and administer a survey in order to collect data on which to make an estimate. Clearly, the figure quoted of 8 000 is an estimate, not an exact figure. After sorting the data it should become clear that it is impossible to arrive at an exact number—the variables are too great. Some children are toilet-trained earlier than others, some wet and mess their nappies more often, some parents use cloth nappies and so on.

Further Investigations

This investigation should prompt the pupils to think of some other data collection exercises such as:
- How much paper is consumed in a school each year?
- How many photocopies are made?

8 000 NAPPIES

 Guideline

? A *Choice* magazine article (August 1999) suggested that by the time a toddler is toilet-trained he/she will have used 8 000 nappies. Another estimate suggested a child would have used 7 000 nappies by the time he/she was toilet-trained.

Which estimate do you think is closer?

_____

Collect some data to answer the question.

Hints and Ideas

By what age is the typical toddler toilet-trained?
I could ask some mums around school.

How many nappy changes does a baby have each day?

Notes and Calculations

Questions

Where will you find the information?

What did you find out?

How will you present your findings?

Findings

www.prim-ed.com – Prim-Ed Publishing   3   **MATHS INVESTIGATIONS**

Teacher Background

The Pencil Case Problem 1

This problem arose because my wife and I chose to call our second son Leighland. Like all teachers, I had trouble coming up with a name that didn't send shivers down my spine every time it was spoken. When Leighland started school, we bought him a pencil case with letter slots for his name. Unfortunately, his name was made up of nine letters and there were only eight slots on the pencil case. This was never a problem for our eldest son Jeremy (so named because of the long vowel sound at the end of his name—handy for yelling over long distances!). It is a fairly simple exercise to collect length of name data in order to check whether eight slots are enough.

Further Investigations

Use the Internet to contact a class from another country and compare the length of names.

THE PENCIL CASE PROBLEM 1

? A pencil case which allows you to place the letters of your name into the slots on the front may be bought from most stationery shops. These pencil cases all come with eight slots into which letters may be placed.

Collect some data to determine whether eight slots are enough for most children to slot in the:

- letters of their first name;
- letters of their surname and first initial;
- letters of their first name and the initial of their surname;
- letters of their nickname.

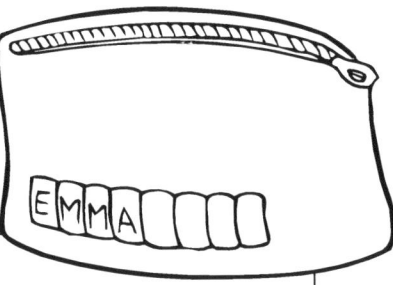

Hints and Ideas

I could collect data from another class to check my findings.

My name is Alexander. It won't fit. I guess I could use Alex.

I'm going to list all the names of nine letters or more that I can think of.

Notes and Calculations

You may wish to collect some data via the Internet to determine how children from other countries would manage.

Questions

Where will you find the information?

What did you find out?

How will you present your findings?

Findings

Teacher

THE PENCIL CASE PROBLEM 2

The problem was tried with a class, which contained quite an ethnic mix, and hence the second pencil case problem arose. The pencil cases come with a set of letters but when the letters are examined more closely, the unusual mix of letters becomes more apparent. For example there are only two As, Is and Os and only one U. Vowels are used in most English words but perhaps the frequency differs in names. A class list provides an excellent opportunity for collecting data as does a Baby Name book.

Further Investigations

The distribution of letters in English may be compared with the distribution in common names. A look at the game of Scrabble also stimulates a great deal of discussion.

THE PENCIL CASE PROBLEM 2

? The same pencil case comes with a set of letters, shown below, which may be cut to fit into the slots.

A	A	B	B	B	C	C	D	D	E	E	E	F	F
G	G	H	H	I	I	J	K	K	L	L	L	M	M
N	N	N	O	O	P	P	Q	R	R	R	S	S	S
T	T	U	V	V	W	X	Y	Z	"	"	!	*	?

Some letters such as E, L, N, R and S feature more often than others.

Collect some data to determine whether the mix of letters is appropriate for most children.

Hints  Ideas

My name is Alana and there aren't enough letter 'A's for me to finish my name.

I wonder why there are only two As, Is, Os and only one U when there are three Bs, Ls, Rs and Ss.

The most commonly used letter of the alphabet is 'e' in the English language, but is this true for names?

Yes ⦃ No

How are the letters distributed in a game of Scrabble?

_____
_____

Notes and Calculations

Questions

Where will you find the information?

What did you find out?

How will you present your findings?

Findings

TEACHER BACKGROUND

TAPE MEASURE

A visit to http://www.pitape.co.uk provides some interesting background to this problem. Any search of the Internet under 'Pi Tape' will bring up similar sites. This problem really tests whether the children understand the c = πd relationship or whether they have rote learnt a formula. If they understand that Pi is about 3 and there is a 3:1 relationship between the diameter and the circumference—producing a tape becomes a fairly simple matter. Roughly every 3 cm or (to be more precise) 3.14 cm, the tape needs to be marked to show a 1-cm diameter division.

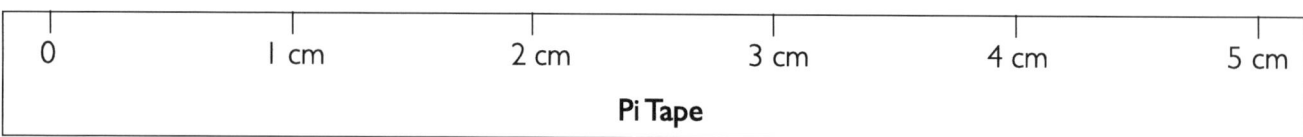

The finished tapes can then be tested on cylindrical objects where the diameter is already known. The need for accuracy may be emphasised by explaining that Pi Tapes are used in the engineering industry—particularly the aircraft and space industry—to accurately measure the diameters of cylindrical parts. These engineers and the pilots and astronauts flying the aircraft need to rely on the accuracy of these measuring devices. The topic of tolerances may also be discussed when producing the tapes.

Further Investigations

A related question involves the production of tennis ball cans. Some tennis ball manufacturers package three tennis balls into a can. If you were to wrap a string around the can and another along the length of the can, which would be longer?

A similar investigation involves measuring the circumference and height of drinking glasses. In most cases you will find the circumference measurement exceeds the height measurement.

TAPE MEASURE

? Design a tape measure that when wrapped around a cylinder could be used to directly read the diameter.

Hints and Ideas

The circumference of a circle is found by multiplying the diameter of the circle by (Pi).

The diameter runs through the middle of a circle.

(Pi) is a little more than three.

Where might a tape like this be used?

It could be used ... .

Who might use such a tape?
_____

Notes and Calculations

Questions

Where will you find the information?

What did you find out?

How will you present your findings?

Findings

MATHS INVESTIGATIONS

Teacher Background

Take a Flying Leap

A quick check of the world record for long jump on the Internet reveals that the record for men is around 8.95 m and for women 7.5 m. The children might like to measure their own attempts at the long jump, which would be significantly shorter than the world record. Buildings on the same block may be closer together than those across the street. Measuring the distance across a road near school will provide a distance that may be used as an approximation in order to answer the question.

TAKE A FLYING LEAP

? Last night on TV I saw a criminal running away from a police officer. They were running across the tops of buildings when they came to the end of the street. The criminal took a flying leap and just managed to make it to the building across the street. The offficer decided not to try. My dad said he was a wimp, but Mum said no-one would be able to jump that far in real life.

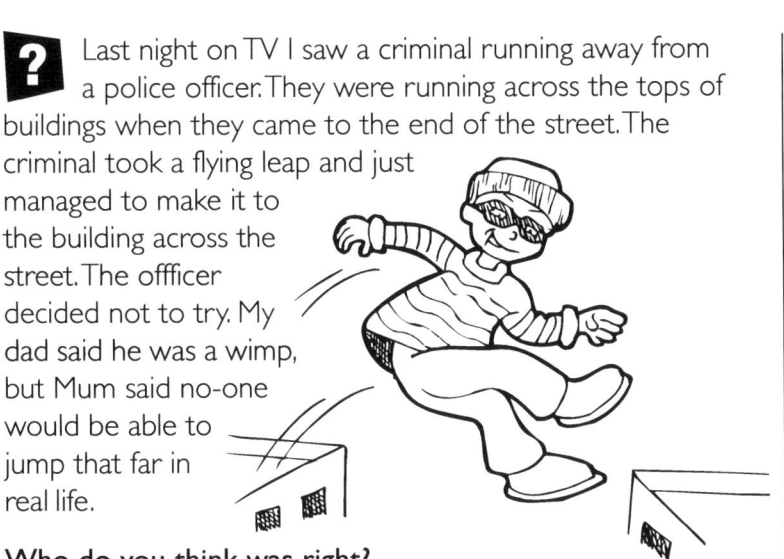

Who do you think was right?

Hints and Ideas

How far can you jump? _____ m

How far is it across an average street?

_____ m

I wonder what would happen if you jumped from a taller building onto a shorter building.

I wonder what the World Record for long jump is.

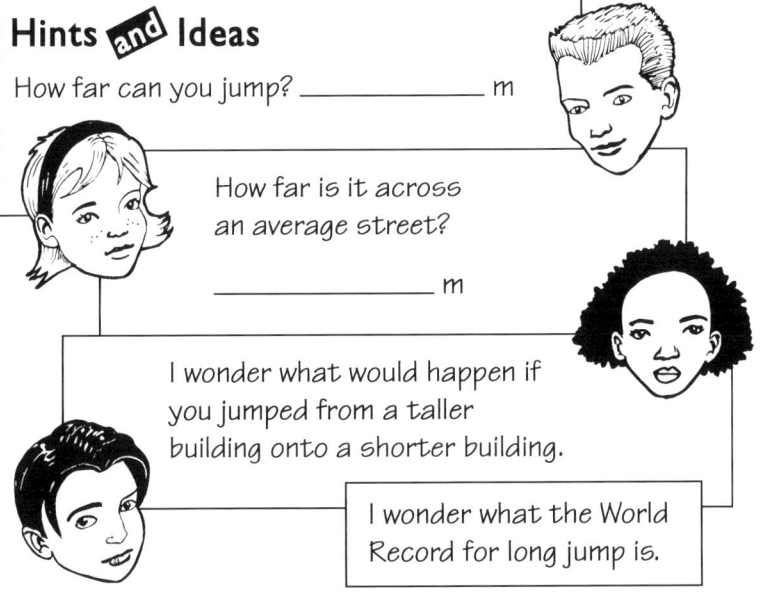

Notes and Calculations

Questions

Where will you find the information?

What did you find out?

How will you present your findings?

Findings

Teacher Background

Big Foot

The footprint used on the Big Foot page belongs to one of my four-year-olds. Collecting foot sizes across several different age groups in the school should provide enough data to note several patterns. One clear pattern is that as a child ages and grows taller, his/her foot size increases. It is highly unlikely that a Year 6 child would have feet as small as the one shown on the page. The children should be able to suggest that the culprit was probably from Year 1.

Further Investigations

Encourage the children to investigate other body measurements. They will need a piece of string as long as their arm span. The children could be encouraged to explore the following relationships.

- Height and arm span – approximately the same.
- Foot length and distance from elbow to wrist.
- Twice around wrist and neck measurement.
- Twice around neck and waist measurement.
- Length of thumb and length of nose.

Be sensitive about taking some body measurements—use discernment.

The data from height and arm span can be used to draw a scattergraph and the relationship or correlation between the two variables may be examined. If correct, the points should be bunched and sloping around a line slanting up from the left to the right.

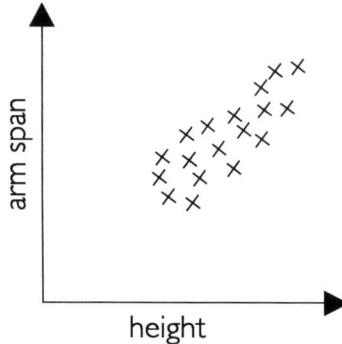

BIG FOOT

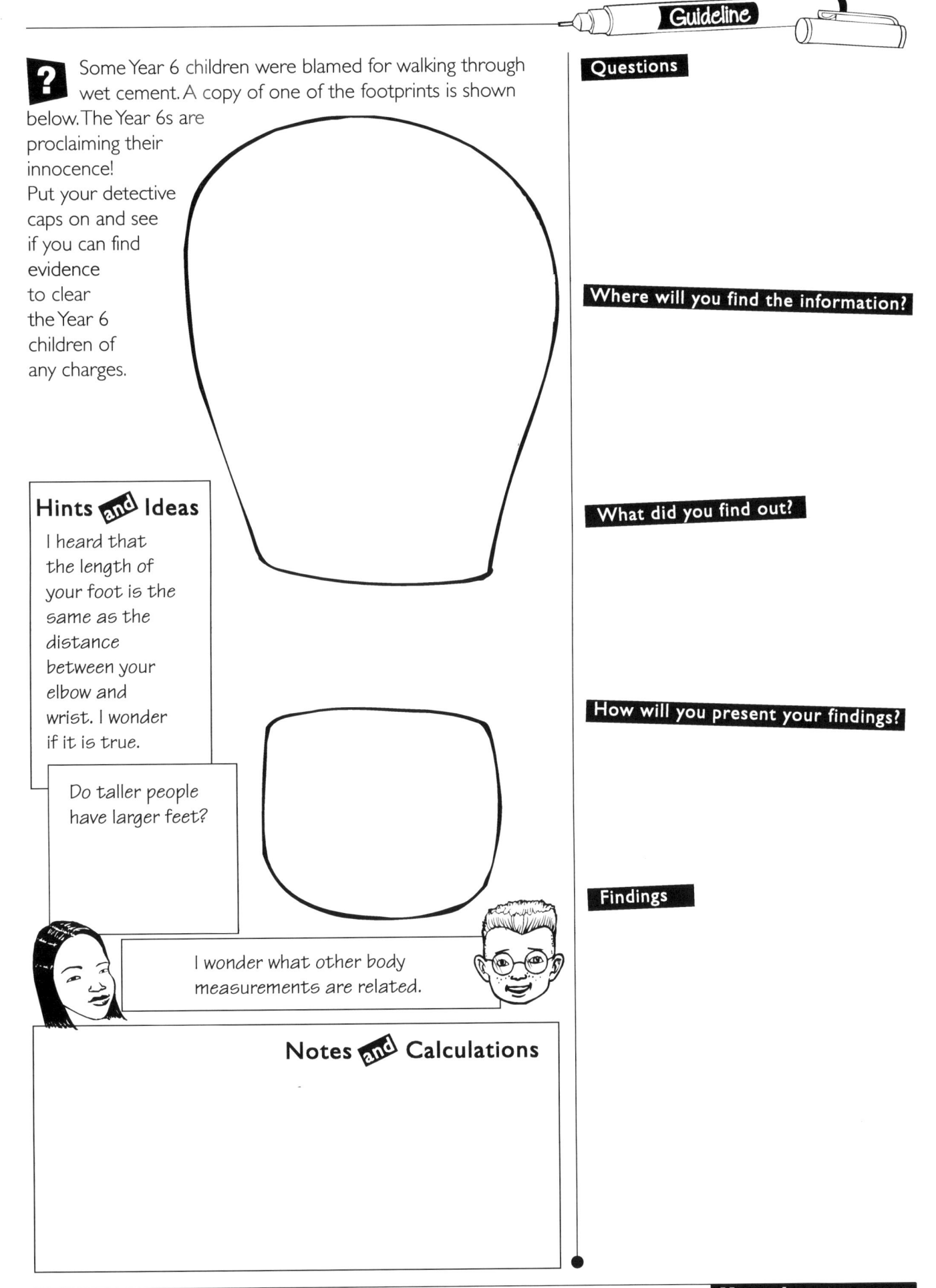

Guideline

? Some Year 6 children were blamed for walking through wet cement. A copy of one of the footprints is shown below. The Year 6s are proclaiming their innocence! Put your detective caps on and see if you can find evidence to clear the Year 6 children of any charges.

Questions

Where will you find the information?

What did you find out?

Hints and Ideas

I heard that the length of your foot is the same as the distance between your elbow and wrist. I wonder if it is true.

Do taller people have larger feet?

How will you present your findings?

I wonder what other body measurements are related.

Findings

Notes and Calculations

www.prim-ed.com – Prim-Ed Publishing   13   **MATHS INVESTIGATIONS**

Teacher Background

Down the Drain

The following facts may add to your discussion:

- Showers use anywhere from 10–20 L of water every minute.
- Most toilets use 12 L of water per flush.
- A dual-flush toilet uses 60 per cent less water.
- Leaving the water running while brushing your teeth wastes 5 L of water.
- A dripping tap can waste 200 L per day.

DOWN THE DRAIN

? A great deal of water is wasted in the home. Did you know that every time you flush the toilet 12 litres of water is used? A leaking tap may also waste thousands of litres of water a year.

How much water do you think the average person uses having a shower?

_____ L

Hints and Ideas

How long do I spend in the shower every day?

How much water flows from the shower head per minute?

We could use a two litre ice-cream container to help us find out.

I wonder if it is more economical to have a bath.

Is it? | Yes | No |

Notes and Calculations

Questions

Where will you find the information?

What did you find out?

How will you present your findings?

Findings

TEACHER BACKGROUND

PIECES OF EIGHT

The most common form of currency used in the early American colonies was a 'piece of eight' or 'Spanish milled dollar'. England did not allow the American colonies to mint their own currency so they adopted the Spanish milled dollar.

The Spanish found precious metals such as gold and silver in Mexico and South America and began establishing mints for making coins. The first mint in America was established by the Spaniards in 1536 in Mexico City, followed soon after by one in South America. The most commonly minted coin was the piece of eight or Spanish milled dollar. The Spanish milled dollar was worth 8 reales and was often cut up into eight pieces—hence the expression 'pieces of eight'. The number 8 was marked on the coin.

The Spanish milled dollar was made of one ounce of silver and had a patterned or 'milled' edge to prevent shaving the edges. Dividing the dollar into eight parts allowed various weights of silver to be produced; e.g. half an ounce, quarter of an ounce and eighth of an ounce. Americans to this day still use the terms 'half' dollar, 'quarter' and 'bits'—12.5c or one-eighth of a whole dollar.

Pirates were always keen to plunder pieces of eight because they were popular in international exchange. The last Spanish milled dollars were minted in 1825 and they continued to be used as legal tender in the USA until 1857. There is evidence of them still circulating in the early part of the twentieth century.

A **gold doubloon** was worth sixteen pieces of eight.

PIECES OF EIGHT

 Guideline

? Last night I watched a pirate movie. The captain was scared that his crew might steal his treasure. While the crew were asleep he carried his treasure chest full of pieces of eight (silver pieces) to the other side of the island he was on and buried it. My sister says there is no way that a person could carry that much on his own. I said pirates were strong. Who was right?

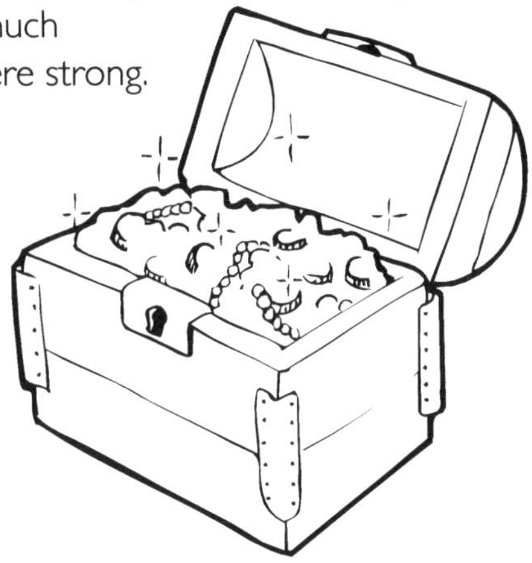

Questions

Hints and Ideas

I wonder how large the treasure chest was.

I wonder how many pieces of eight would fit into the treasure chest.

Maybe we could try £1 and £2 coins to test our ideas.

Could the pirate carry the chest if it was filled with gold doubloons?

What were gold doubloons?

How much did a piece of eight weigh?

Where will you find the information?

What did you find out?

How will you present your findings?

Notes and Calculations

Findings

www.prim-ed.com – Prim-Ed Publishing 17 MATHS INVESTIGATIONS

Teacher Background

THE MONEY TRAIL

The Money Trail and The Concert Queue provide a wonderful opportunity for discussion. At first glance a child might assume that a money trail of 20p coins would have twice the value of a trail made up of 10p coins but because the 20p coin is smaller there would be more 20p coins in a money trail (assuming the lengths were the same). A 20p coin money trail would therefore have a value more than twice a 10p coin money trail.

The Money Trail requires the use of measurement and computation skills whereas the Concert Queue problem is more sophisticated. The Concert Queue involves a certain amount of estimation as the distance between people in a concert queue will vary. Friends may be queued up side by side. Some people might prefer more personal space and so on, therefore various assumptions have to be made; e.g. use of a newspaper page as the equivalent of space required by one person. The final result can therefore only be an estimate—so an answer of 463 people is only representative of a range of people possibly between 400 and 500 people. This provides an ideal opportunity to discuss **estimates, ranges, assumptions and tolerances.**

Further Investigations

The opportunity to discuss how organisations deal with queues may also arise; e.g.

- why do queues at airports zigzag?; or
- the use of multiple queues and turnstiles.

THE MONEY TRAIL

 Guideline

? To raise money for new playground equipment, the children of a local primary school put on a concert and asked the audience to bring a silver coin donation. The money was placed in a trail that reached 100 m across the playground.

How much money might have been raised? _____

Hints and Ideas

Would you raise twice as much if you asked for 20p coins instead of 10p coins?

If everyone brought 10p coins, how many were in the audience?

If half the audience brought 10p and half the audience brought 20p coins, how much would have been raised?

What would happen if a gold coin donation was suggested rather than a silver coin?

Last night on the news, hundreds of people were shown lining up for concert tickets. The queue was so long that it reached 1 km down the street.

How many people do you estimate were in the queue?

_____

How far does the line extend when the class lines up?

I thought I might use a piece of newspaper to help me. I think one person needs about one sheet of newspaper space in a queue.

Notes and Calculations

Questions

Where will you find the information?

What did you find out?

How will you present your findings?

Findings

---

www.prim-ed.com – Prim-Ed Publishing   19   **MATHS INVESTIGATIONS**

TEACHER BACKGROUND

COMPETITION MATHS

The solution to the CD problem involves measuring the height of a CD in its cover and measuring the heights of various members of the class. Children can find an **average or mean CD price** to determine the value of the prize. Many of the same techniques may be used to investigate the video/DVD option. Obviously a video cassette option would be cheaper because, when packed in covers, video cassettes are much thicker than a DVD. The worst case scenario would involve an extremely tall person (children could look up the Guinness Book of World Records) winning his/her height in DVDs.

The problem with running a similar competition using books is that the thickness of different books can vary.

Further Investigations

Children can research the tallest man who ever lived by looking at the following websites:

http://www.altonweb.com/history/wadlow/

http://www.roadsideamerica.com/attract/ILALTwadlow.html

Note: Discussion about the CD competition might be stimulated by bringing in a stack of CDs and asking the students to estimate the worth of the collection.

COMPETITION MATHS

? Radio stations often run competitions where the prize involves winning a stack of CDs the same height as the winner.

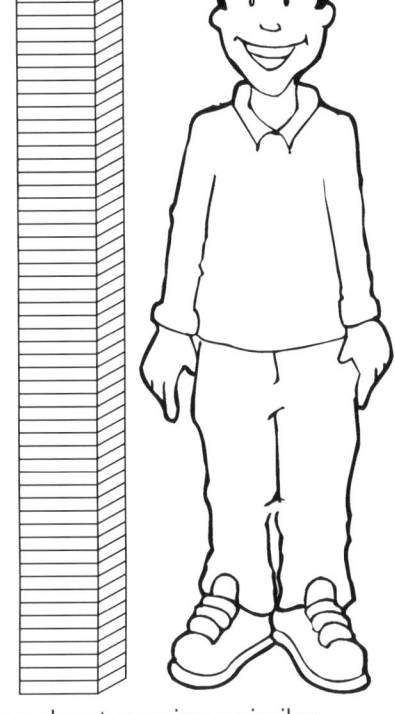

Hints and Ideas

How many CDs would you get if you won?
_____

How thick is a CD?

How much do CDs cost?

How much would the prize be worth?
_____

The local video shop is thinking about running a similar competition using videos or DVDs or perhaps a mix of each. Write a report outlining your suggestions for the competition. You might like to consider various options and the 'worst case scenario' (for example, if a really tall person won).

Notes and Calculations

My Report

Questions

Where to find answers

Data collected

Advice to local video shop

The local bookstore is also considering a similar competition where the winner would receive a stack of books to match his/her height. What problems might occur if books were the prizes?
_____
_____
_____

www.prim-ed.com – Prim-Ed Publishing   21   **MATHS INVESTIGATIONS**

TEACHER BACKGROUND

CROSSING THE ROAD

Most of us have been caught short crossing the road at pedestrian crossings where the 'red man' sign starts flashing when we are only halfway across the road.

Children will need to collect data such as:

- What is the width of a single lane and double lane road?
- How fast does the average person walk?
- How fast does a senior citizen walk?
- How long does the signal allow for crossing the road?

A letter to or Internet search of the local council or Department of Transport will provide data on crossing times.

CROSSING THE ROAD

Guideline

? Some traffic signals include walk signs which indicate when it is safe to cross the road. The green walk signals are set on a timer which often makes a beeping noise prior to flashing a warning.

Collect data to determine how much time should be allowed for the 'average' person to cross the road.

Hints and Ideas

How wide is a road with traffic lights?

What about older people, people with prams and little children?

How fast does a person walk?

Notes and Calculations

Questions

Where will you find the information?

What did you find out?

How will you present your findings?

Findings

Teacher Background

TINKERING WITH TIME

Much of our 'time' work with children involves learning how to read the time from a clockface. This activity focuses on the **passage of time**; i.e. gaining a feel for time. Children's concept of time passing is affected by events, such as waiting for the day of a party to come (time seems to drag). Parents often use the expression 'wait a sec' or 'I'll only be 5 minutes'—and half an hour later a child is still waiting.

The study of **horology** is fascinating and there are many websites based on the development of accurate measuring devices for time. If children are given the opportunity to 'invent' a device for measuring a set amount of time they will gain a better appreciation for the struggle to measure time. Nowadays we take the clock on the wall or the watch on our wrist for granted.

Hints and Ideas

There is a wealth of information to be found on the Internet under headings such as horology, clepsydra (water clock), sundial, hourglass and so on. The pendulum, still found in clocks today, was initially discovered by Galileo (as the story goes) when he was bored in church one day. He noticed a lamp swinging in the cathedral and began to time the swings using his pulse or heartbeat as the measure. He discovered that the time it took to go back and forth was the same regardless of the size of the swing.

When experimenting with a pendulum, children should come to the realisation that the period of the pendulum is independent of the mass of the weight on the end. However, changing the length of the string will affect the period of the pendulum.

TINKERING WITH TIME

Guideline

? Many people have developed ways of estimating the passage of time. For example, to estimate how many seconds have passed, some people count '1 000 and 2 000 and 3 000 and 4 000' and so on, depending on the number of seconds.

Throughout the ages various devices have been used to measure time. For example, time has been measured using candle clocks, sand timers and water clocks. Use some of the materials listed below to make a device to measure a set number of seconds.

Materials List

plastic drink containers, plastic cup, rice, sand, marbles, plastic pipe, candle, string, washers and weights

Hints and Ideas

I could research the use of water, sand and candle clocks to measure time.

What is a pendulum?

You can make a pendulum using a string and a weight.

I count one elephant, two elephants, three elephants and so on.

A famous mathematician called Galileo investigated the use of pendulums to measure time.

Some clocks have a pendulum which swings below the clock.

What happens when you vary the length of the string? Does a heavier or lighter weight affect the pendulum?

My diagram

How it works

_____
_____
_____
_____
_____
_____
_____
_____

Does it work? Yes / No

Notes and Calculations

TEACHER BACKGROUND

METRIC TIME

With the advent of hundredths of a second, **milliseconds** and even **nanoseconds** one could be forgiven for thinking that time was already based on powers of ten. Our system of measuring time appears to have begun thousands of years ago with the Sumerians who used a counting system based on 60, hence 60 seconds in a minute and 60 minutes in an hour. Several ancient societies used a **duodecimal system** (one based on 12 – we still use a dozen when buying certain items like eggs) and hence 12 became significant in the keeping of time. Note: At one time there were only 12 hours in a day (longer than the hour used today).

Further Investigations

For further background reading on the development of time see:

Waugh, A. (1999), Time: From micro-seconds to millenia – a search for the right time, Headline Publishing, London.

Metric Time

? Most countries use the metric system for measurement. The units in this system are all related by multiples of ten. For example, there are 1 000 mm in a metre and 100 cm in a metre.

When it comes to measuring time, however, the system is a mess. Twenty-four hours make one day, there are 60 minutes in one hour and so on.

Design a 'metric' system for measuring time.

Hints and Ideas

How did they come up with the metric system?

I heard it came from France.

One book I read said the standard for the metre was changed in the twentieth century. I wonder if that is true.

Notes and Calculations

Questions

Where will you find the information?

What did you find out?

How will you present your findings?

Findings

MATHS INVESTIGATIONS

TEACHER

CALENDAR CORRECTIONS

The calendar has undergone many changes and corrections over the centuries. One of the most dramatic was the change from the **Julian Calendar** to the **Gregorian Calendar** in 1582. The Gregorian Calendar, which is still currently in use, includes the concept of a **leap year**, which the Julian Calendar did not. A leap year is required because a year is made up of 365.24 days, so every fourth year is given an extra day to compensate for the 0.24 extra part each year. Note: 4 x 0.24 does not equal a whole day, hence the rule that a leap year does not occur at the turn of the century unless the century is divisible by four without leaving a remainder; e.g. 1600, 2000. Note: 1900 and 1800 were not leap years.

The Julian Calendar was replaced by the Gregorian Calendar on 4 October, 1582 in Catholic countries. People went to bed on 4 October and woke up on 15 October. Many non-Catholic countries chose not to change their calendar. It wasn't until the twentieth century that the final few countries changed over. Even today, some history books will list two dates for particular historical events—one date using the Julian Calendar and the other using the Gregorian Calendar.

For further information see page 30.

CALENDAR CORRECTIONS

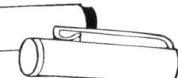 Guideline

Questions

? Have you ever wondered why the tenth month of the year is called October when 'Oct' means eight? Most people have to recite a little poem to remember the number of days in a particular month. What a mess!

Redesign the calendar to make it simple to use.

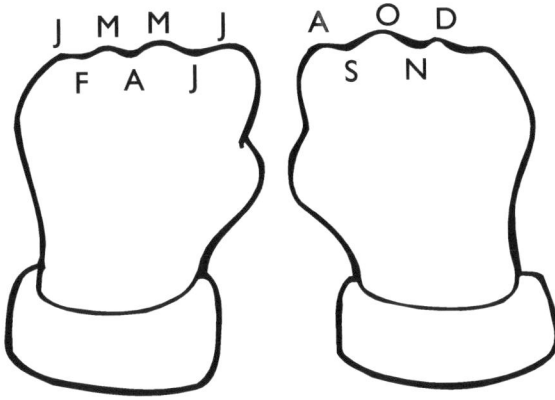

Where will you find the information?

Hints and Ideas

30 days has September, April, June and November. All the rest have 31, except February.
I wonder why some months have 31 days and poor old February only has 28.

If there are 52 weeks in a year and 7 days in a week, why are there 365 days in a year and not 364?

I use my knuckles to work out how many days in each month.

A leap year is used to keep the calendar in order. Why was the year 2000 a leap year but not 1900?

What did you find out?

Notes and Calculations

How will you present your findings?

Findings

www.prim-ed.com – Prim-Ed Publishing 29 **MATHS INVESTIGATIONS**

Teacher Background

THE WORLD CALENDAR

The upheaval caused by another change in the calendar would be so great that people the world over have resisted the temptation to change, even though several proposals have been put forward. Probably the most interesting proposal goes under the title of:

The World Calendar

A search of the World Wide Web under 'World Calendar' will bring up some interesting background information. You may like to show a copy to your children to see whether they can list any advantages and disadvantages to adopting this calendar.

The calendar affects our lives in many different ways and children need to gain an appreciation of the role that the calendar plays in society. Children should also realise that the Gregorian Calendar is not the only one in use. Consider, for example, the Jewish Calendar, the Chinese Calendar and the Buddhist Calendar. Apparently the Balinese operate two calendars besides the Gregorian Calendar. One calendar is to keep track of religious festivals.

A World Calendar is shown on page 31.

Ask the children to explain what they notice about the World Calendar (i.e. any patterns).

THE WORLD CALENDAR

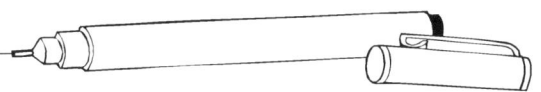

First Quarter

January
S	M	T	W	T	F	S
1	2	3	4	5	6	7
8	9	10	11	12	13	14
15	16	17	18	19	20	21
22	23	24	25	26	27	28
29	30	31				

February
S	M	T	W	T	F	S
				1	2	3	4
5	6	7	8	9	10	11
12	13	14	15	16	17	18
19	20	21	22	23	24	25
26	27	28	29	30		

March
S	M	T	W	T	F	S
					1	2
3	4	5	6	7	8	9
10	11	12	13	14	15	16
17	18	19	20	21	22	23
24	25	26	27	28	29	30

Second Quarter

April
S	M	T	W	T	F	S
1	2	3	4	5	6	7
8	9	10	11	12	13	14
15	16	17	18	19	20	21
22	23	24	25	26	27	28
29	30	31				

May
S	M	T	W	T	F	S
				1	2	3	4
5	6	7	8	9	10	11
12	13	14	15	16	17	18
19	20	21	22	23	24	25
26	27	28	29	30		

June
S	M	T	W	T	F	S
					1	2
3	4	5	6	7	8	9
10	11	12	13	14	15	16
17	18	19	20	21	22	23
24	25	26	27	28	29	30	W

Third Quarter

July
S	M	T	W	T	F	S
1	2	3	4	5	6	7
8	9	10	11	12	13	14
15	16	17	18	19	20	21
22	23	24	25	26	27	28
29	30	31				

August
S	M	T	W	T	F	S
				1	2	3	4
5	6	7	8	9	10	11
12	13	14	15	16	17	18
19	20	21	22	23	24	25
26	27	28	29	30		

September
S	M	T	W	T	F	S
					1	2
3	4	5	6	7	8	9
10	11	12	13	14	15	16
17	18	19	20	21	22	23
24	25	26	27	28	29	30

Fourth Quarter

October
S	M	T	W	T	F	S
1	2	3	4	5	6	7
8	9	10	11	12	13	14
15	16	17	18	19	20	21
22	23	24	25	26	27	28
29	30	31				

November
S	M	T	W	T	F	S
				1	2	3	4
5	6	7	8	9	10	11
12	13	14	15	16	17	18
19	20	21	22	23	24	25
26	27	28	29	30		

December
S	M	T	W	T	F	S
					1	2
3	4	5	6	7	8	9
10	11	12	13	14	15	16
17	18	19	20	21	22	23
24	25	26	27	28	29	30	W*

W = Leap Year Day, World Holiday (183rd day), outside the week.

W* = Worldsday, World Holiday (365th day), outside the week.

Teacher Background

THE CALENDAR

The current calendar we use is called a **Gregorian Calendar**, dating back to Pope Gregory. It is an **annual calendar** in that it changes each year. The reason it changes each year is because the 365 days that make up a year are not divisible by 7 without leaving a remainder. Note: When you divide 365 by 7 there is a remainder of one—hence each year starts and finishes on the same day and the next year will begin on the next day of the week. The overall consequence of this is that seven different calendars are required to cover all possible starting days. A further *seven calendars are required to cope with leap years*, which may begin on any day of the week. In total 14 calendars are needed to cover all possibilities.

Four consecutive calendar years can be seen on page 35.

THE CALENDAR

Guideline

? My mother has a tea towel with last year's calendar printed on it. When I was washing up I compared the calendar for last year with the new calendar for this year. I noticed that my birthday is on a different day this year. Last year my birthday was on a Wednesday. This year my birthday is on a Thursday. Looking at the calendar printed on the tea towel I began to wonder …

When might we be able to use the same calendar again?

(Our calendar is an annual calendar. It changes every year.)

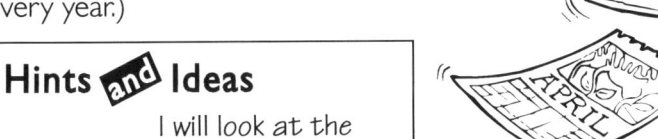

Hints and Ideas

- I will look at the calendars for four consecutive years.
- On which day does this year begin and end?
- I wonder what happens in a leap year.

How many different calendars would you need to produce to cover all possibilities?

Hints and Ideas

- What happens to your birthday in a leap year?
- Does it matter whether your birthday falls before or after February 29?
- I wonder what happens if you were born on February 29.

Notes and Calculations

A character called Frederic in 'The Pirates of Penzance' by Gilbert and Sullivan turned 21 after only 5 birthdays. Explain how this was the case.

Questions

Where will you find the information?

What did you find out?

How will you present your findings?

Findings

Teacher Background

Four Calendars

To be used with the activity on page 33, The Calendar.

Four Calendars

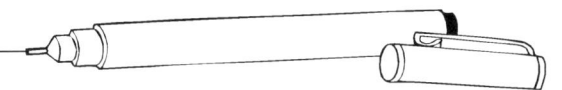

* 2004 is a leap year.

2002

January
M	T	W	T	F	S	S
	1	2	3	4	5	6
7	8	9	10	11	12	13
14	15	16	17	18	19	20
21	22	23	24	25	26	27
28	29	30	31			

February
M	T	W	T	F	S	S
				1	2	3
4	5	6	7	8	9	10
11	12	13	14	15	16	17
18	19	20	21	22	23	24
25	26	27	28			

March
M	T	W	T	F	S	S
				1	2	3
4	5	6	7	8	9	10
11	12	13	14	15	16	17
18	19	20	21	22	23	24
25	26	27	28	29	30	31

April
M	T	W	T	F	S	S
1	2	3	4	5	6	7
8	9	10	11	12	13	14
15	16	17	18	19	20	21
22	23	24	25	26	27	28
29	30					

May
M	T	W	T	F	S	S
		1	2	3	4	5
6	7	8	9	10	11	12
13	14	15	16	17	18	19
20	21	22	23	24	25	26
27	28	29	30	31		

June
M	T	W	T	F	S	S
					1	2
3	4	5	6	7	8	9
10	11	12	13	14	15	16
17	18	19	20	21	22	23
24	25	26	27	28	29	30

July
M	T	W	T	F	S	S
1	2	3	4	5	6	7
8	9	10	11	12	13	14
15	16	17	18	19	20	21
22	23	24	25	26	27	28
29	30	31				

August
M	T	W	T	F	S	S
			1	2	3	4
5	6	7	8	9	10	11
12	13	14	15	16	17	18
19	20	21	22	23	24	25
26	27	28	29	30	31	

September
M	T	W	T	F	S	S
30						1
2	3	4	5	6	7	8
9	10	11	12	13	14	15
16	17	18	19	20	21	22
23	24	25	26	27	28	29

October
M	T	W	T	F	S	S
	1	2	3	4	5	6
7	8	9	10	11	12	13
14	15	16	17	18	19	20
21	22	23	24	25	26	27
28	29	30	31			

November
M	T	W	T	F	S	S
				1	2	3
4	5	6	7	8	9	10
11	12	13	14	15	16	17
18	19	20	21	22	23	24
25	26	27	28	29	30	

December
M	T	W	T	F	S	S
30	31					1
2	3	4	5	6	7	8
9	10	11	12	13	14	15
16	17	18	19	20	21	22
23	24	25	26	27	28	29

2003

January
M	T	W	T	F	S	S
	1	2	3	4	5	
6	7	8	9	10	11	12
13	14	15	16	17	18	19
20	21	22	23	24	25	26
27	28	29	30	31		

February
M	T	W	T	F	S	S
					1	2
3	4	5	6	7	8	9
10	11	12	13	14	15	16
17	18	19	20	21	22	23
24	25	26	27	28		

March
M	T	W	T	F	S	S
31					1	2
3	4	5	6	7	8	9
10	11	12	13	14	15	16
17	18	19	20	21	22	23
24	25	26	27	28	29	30

April
M	T	W	T	F	S	S
	1	2	3	4	5	6
7	8	9	10	11	12	13
14	15	16	17	18	19	20
21	22	23	24	25	26	27
28	29	30				

May
M	T	W	T	F	S	S
			1	2	3	4
5	6	7	8	9	10	11
12	13	14	15	16	17	18
19	20	21	22	23	24	25
26	27	28	29	30	31	

June
M	T	W	T	F	S	S
30						1
2	3	4	5	6	7	8
9	10	11	12	13	14	15
16	17	18	19	20	21	22
23	24	25	26	27	28	29

July
M	T	W	T	F	S	S
	1	2	3	4	5	6
7	8	9	10	11	12	13
14	15	16	17	18	19	20
21	22	23	24	25	26	27
28	29	30	31			

August
M	T	W	T	F	S	S
				1	2	3
4	5	6	7	8	9	10
11	12	13	14	15	16	17
18	19	20	21	22	23	24
25	26	27	28	29	30	31

September
M	T	W	T	F	S	S
1	2	3	4	5	6	7
8	9	10	11	12	13	14
15	16	17	18	19	20	21
22	23	24	25	26	27	28
29	30					

October
M	T	W	T	F	S	S
		1	2	3	4	5
6	7	8	9	10	11	12
13	14	15	16	17	18	19
20	21	22	23	24	25	26
27	28	29	30	31		

November
M	T	W	T	F	S	S
					1	2
3	4	5	6	7	8	9
10	11	12	13	14	15	16
17	18	19	20	21	22	23
24	25	26	27	28	29	30

December
M	T	W	T	F	S	S
1	2	3	4	5	6	7
8	9	10	11	12	13	14
15	16	17	18	19	20	21
22	23	24	25	26	27	28
29	30	31				

2004*

January
M	T	W	T	F	S	S
			1	2	3	4
5	6	7	8	9	10	11
12	13	14	15	16	17	18
19	20	21	22	23	24	25
26	27	28	29	30	31	

February
M	T	W	T	F	S	S
						1
2	3	4	5	6	7	8
9	10	11	12	13	14	15
16	17	18	19	20	21	22
23	24	25	26	27	28	29

March
M	T	W	T	F	S	S
1	2	3	4	5	6	7
8	9	10	11	12	13	14
15	16	17	18	19	20	21
22	23	24	25	26	27	28
29	30	31				

April
M	T	W	T	F	S	S
			1	2	3	4
5	6	7	8	9	10	11
12	13	14	15	16	17	18
19	20	21	22	23	24	25
26	27	28	29	30		

May
M	T	W	T	F	S	S
31					1	2
3	4	5	6	7	8	9
10	11	12	13	14	15	16
17	18	19	20	21	22	23
24	25	26	27	28	29	30

June
M	T	W	T	F	S	S
	1	2	3	4	5	6
7	8	9	10	11	12	13
14	15	16	17	18	19	20
21	22	23	24	25	26	27
28	29	30				

July
M	T	W	T	F	S	S
			1	2	3	4
5	6	7	8	9	10	11
12	13	14	15	16	17	18
19	20	21	22	23	24	25
26	27	28	29	30	31	

August
M	T	W	T	F	S	S
30	31					1
2	3	4	5	6	7	8
9	10	11	12	13	14	15
16	17	18	19	20	21	22
23	24	25	26	27	28	29

September
M	T	W	T	F	S	S
		1	2	3	4	5
6	7	8	9	10	11	12
13	14	15	16	17	18	19
20	21	22	23	24	25	26
27	28	29	30			

October
M	T	W	T	F	S	S
				1	2	3
4	5	6	7	8	9	10
11	12	13	14	15	16	17
18	19	20	21	22	23	24
25	26	27	28	29	30	31

November
M	T	W	T	F	S	S
1	2	3	4	5	6	7
8	9	10	11	12	13	14
15	16	17	18	19	20	21
22	23	24	25	26	27	28
29	30					

December
M	T	W	T	F	S	S
		1	2	3	4	5
6	7	8	9	10	11	12
13	14	15	16	17	18	19
20	21	22	23	24	25	26
27	28	29	30	31		

2005

January
M	T	W	T	F	S	S
31					1	2
3	4	5	6	7	8	9
10	11	12	13	14	15	16
17	18	19	20	21	22	23
24	25	26	27	28	29	30

February
M	T	W	T	F	S	S
	1	2	3	4	5	6
7	8	9	10	11	12	13
14	15	16	17	18	19	20
21	22	23	24	25	26	27
28						

March
M	T	W	T	F	S	S
	1	2	3	4	5	6
7	8	9	10	11	12	13
14	15	16	17	18	19	20
21	22	23	24	25	26	27
28	29	30	31			

April
M	T	W	T	F	S	S
				1	2	3
4	5	6	7	8	9	10
11	12	13	14	15	16	17
18	19	20	21	22	23	24
25	26	27	28	29	30	

May
M	T	W	T	F	S	S
30	31					1
2	3	4	5	6	7	8
9	10	11	12	13	14	15
16	17	18	19	20	21	22
23	24	25	26	27	28	29

June
M	T	W	T	F	S	S
		1	2	3	4	5
6	7	8	9	10	11	12
13	14	15	16	17	18	19
20	21	22	23	24	25	26
27	28	29	30			

July
M	T	W	T	F	S	S
				1	2	3
4	5	6	7	8	9	10
11	12	13	14	15	16	17
18	19	20	21	22	23	24
25	26	27	28	29	30	31

August
M	T	W	T	F	S	S
1	2	3	4	5	6	7
8	9	10	11	12	13	14
15	16	17	18	19	20	21
22	23	24	25	26	27	28
29	30	31				

September
M	T	W	T	F	S	S
			1	2	3	4
5	6	7	8	9	10	11
12	13	14	15	16	17	18
19	20	21	22	23	24	25
26	27	28	29	30		

October
M	T	W	T	F	S	S
31					1	2
3	4	5	6	7	8	9
10	11	12	13	14	15	16
17	18	19	20	21	22	23
24	25	26	27	28	29	30

November
M	T	W	T	F	S	S
	1	2	3	4	5	6
7	8	9	10	11	12	13
14	15	16	17	18	19	20
21	22	23	24	25	26	27
28	29	30				

December
M	T	W	T	F	S	S
			1	2	3	4
5	6	7	8	9	10	11
12	13	14	15	16	17	18
19	20	21	22	23	24	25
26	27	28	29	30	31	

www.prim-ed.com – Prim-Ed Publishing

MATHS INVESTIGATIONS

TEACHER
Background
CALENDAR CONUNDRUMS

The library and the Internet contain a great deal of information about different cultures and the calendars they use. Many cultures use two calendars—the Gregorian, which most Western societies use, and their own. Most business is conducted according to the **Gregorian Calendar** but religious festivals and celebrations are measured against traditional calendars. The Jewish and Buddhist calendars do not measure dates from the birth of Christ. The year number on the Jewish Calendar represents the number of years since creation. This was determined by adding all the ages of the people in the Bible back to the beginning. The Jewish Calendar is a **lunar calendar**. *Each new month begins on the new moon.* The problem with a lunar calendar is that the 12 months are too short (11 days are lost each year) and 13 months are too long (19 days are gained each year). Trying to match the lunar calendar and the Gregorian Calendar is the reason why the dates for certain religious ceremonies seem to change each year.

Most Buddhist calendars begin with Buddha's death, so the year 2002 is the year 2545 on the Buddhist Calendar.

Some useful calendar facts
The names of the months

January	Janus	a two-faced god who looked back on the old year and forward to the new year
February	Februa	the name of a festival held in that month
March	Mars	god of war
April	Aperio	means to open – spring flowers bloom
May	Maia	goddess of spring, growth
June	Juno	goddess of marriage
July	Julius	Caesar
August	Augustus	Caesar
September		Roman for seven
October		Roman for eight
November		Roman for nine
December		Roman for ten

Originally the year started in March and there were only ten months. January and February were added later. Each month consisted of 29 days and the year was only 290 days long!

The Jewish Calendar has the following months:

Name	Number	Length	Gregorian Equivalent
Nissan	1	30 days	March – April
Iyar	2	29 days	April – May
Sivan	3	30 days	May – June
Tammuz	4	29 days	June – July
Av	5	30 days	July – August
Elul	6	29 days	August – September
Tishri	7	30 days	September – October
Cheshvan	8	29 or 30 days	October – November
Kislev	9	30 or 29 days	November – December
Tevet	10	29 days	December – January
Shevat	11	30 days	January – February
Adar	12	29 or 30 days	February – March
Adar II	13	29 days	March – April

In leap years, Adar has 30 days. In non-leap years, Adar has 29 days.

Maths Investigations

CALENDAR CONUNDRUMS

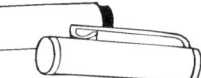

Guideline

? Imagine life without a calendar. What would change in your life? What would stay the same?

Questions

Change	Stay the same

Choose a research topic from the list below and present your findings to the class as a poster or report.

- What is the difference between a lunar and solar calendar?
- The Chinese Calendar
- The Jewish Calendar
- How the days were named
- How the months were named
- The Julian Calendar
- The Gregorian Calendar
- What do the abbreviations a.m., p.m., BC, AD, CE, BCE mean?
- Why does the date for Easter change each year?

Where will you find the information?

Hints and Ideas

How would I know when the holidays start?

I could be in Year 6 at school forever without a calendar.

Did you know the year 46 BC was 455 days long?

At least I wouldn't have to learn dates in history.

You didn't know the Egyptian year only had three seasons—the sowing, the growing and the flooding season!

There are many different calendars in use today besides the one we commonly use.

Did you know that in 1752 the start of the year was moved to 1 January?

What did you find out?

How will you present your findings?

Notes and Calculations

Findings

Present your findings to the class.

MATHS INVESTIGATIONS

Teacher Background

WRITING A MILLION

Mike Dolega finished writing the numbers from 1 to 1 000 000 on 19 February 1989. The Australian man had spent 1 282 hours and used 97 ballpoint pens to fill the 40, 96-page exercise books. The process lasted over two years and has given Mike an appreciation of how many a million really is!

Further Investigations

The book **Counting on Frank** (The Learning Company/Creative Wonders, 1994) by Rod Clemments includes plenty of opportunities for children to estimate and experience working with large numbers. I have even heard of one group of children who, after reading the passage on the amount of ink in a ballpoint pen, tested the length of a line that could be drawn before the ink ran out. Consider how you would design such an experiment.

The Story of Gauss

Children could be told the story of Gauss—a famous mathematician who, at the age of 10, was punished for being naughty in class. The teacher told him to add all the numbers from 1 to 100. Most people would think that this punishment would take a long time to complete, so imagine the teacher's surprise when young Gauss finished the punishment in just a few minutes. Children should be given the opportunity to try the problem before explaining that he saw a pattern when the numbers were paired. The approach Gauss used may be illustrated using the numbers 1 to 10.

$$1 + 2 + 3 + 4 + 5 + 6 + 7 + 8 + 9 + 10$$

Each pair of numbers adds to 11 and there five pairs, hence the total is 55.

Writing a Million

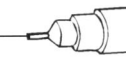

Guideline

? Questions

nine hundred and ninety-nine thousand, nine hundred and ninety-seven;
nine hundred and ninety-nine thousand, nine hundred and ninety-eight;
nine hundred and ninety-nine thousand, nine hundred and ninety-nine;
one million!

Imagine writing all the numbers from one to a million!

How many pages of paper do you think you would use?

Explain how you arrived at your estimate.

Where will you find the information?

Hints and Ideas

I think it would depend on whether the numbers were written as words or numerals.

I once heard of a teacher punishing a child by asking him to add all the numbers from one to a hundred.

I heard he was able to add all the numbers from 1–100 in just a few seconds.

I wonder how he did it so quickly. It would take me ages!

What did you find out?

How will you present your findings?

Notes and Calculations

Findings

You might be surprised to learn that an Australian man, Mike Dolega, actually wrote all the numbers from 1 to 1 000 000.

www.prim-ed.com – Prim-Ed Publishing   39   **MATHS INVESTIGATIONS**

TEACHER BACKGROUND

TYPING A MILLION

Les Stewart from Australia is cited in the Guinness Book of World Records as holding the record for 'Typing Numbers in Words'. He began typing in 1982 and finished 16 years, seven months later. He managed to complete around three pages a day by typing for 20 minutes per hour.

Note, he typed using one finger and used seven typewriters and 1 000 ribbons. All in all he used up 19 890 pages of paper. See **http://www.recordholders.org/en/records/typing.html**

To estimate how long this task would take, children need to time how long it takes to type numbers in words. Obviously, it is fairly quick to type the number 'six' but it would take a great deal more time to type nine hundred and ninety-nine thousand, nine hundred and ninety-seven. The children would need to type a variety of numbers to form an 'average' or 'mean' typing time.

When calculating the number of pages required, children should use a plain font such as Courier as this is closer to the original typewriter print. A picture of a typed page is shown on the website. This will give some indication of the spacing used.

Note: Having been brought up with computers and word processors, most children will not be familiar with mechanical or electrical typewriters, so they may not be aware of the reason behind the placement of keys on the standard 'QWERTY' keyboard. Basically, the keys were placed this way in order to slow down typists who were jamming the mechanical keys on the typewriter because they were typing too fast. In this day of word processors and computers, why is the same keyboard layout still used? Children might like to investigate alternative keyboard layouts by searching the Internet.

Typing a Million

Guideline

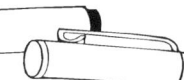

? nine hundred and ninety-nine thousand, nine hundred and ninety-seven; nine hundred and ninety-nine thousand, nine hundred and ninety-eight; nine hundred and ninety-nine thousand, nine hundred and ninety-nine; one million!

Imagine typing all the numbers from one to a million!

You might be surprised to learn that an Australian, Les Stewart, holds the world record for typing numbers. He used a manual typewriter and only one finger to press the keys.

Estimate how long you think this task would take. _____

Estimate how many pages of paper would be used. _____

How did you arrive at your estimates? _____

Hints and Ideas

- Sounds like a new type of punishment that a teacher dreamt up.
- It would take years to type all those numbers!
- Remember you couldn't type all day every day.
- How many lines can be typed onto a single page?
- As the numbers become larger there are more letters to type.

Notes and Calculations

Questions

Where will you find the information?

What did you find out?

How will you present your findings?

Findings

www.prim-ed.com – Prim-Ed Publishing   41   MATHS INVESTIGATIONS

TEACHER BACKGROUND

A FEEL FOR BIG NUMBERS

Children are often fascinated by large numbers. This stimulus page, along with A Million Dots, is designed to capitalise on this interest. News reports often refer to numbers in the billions and sometimes trillions and yet these numbers are meaningless unless we have some idea of their size.

The question 'Have you lived for a million seconds?' is designed to show how a million 'small things' soon add up.

1 000 000 ÷ 60 ÷ 60 ÷ 24 shows that one million seconds is slightly over $11\frac{1}{2}$ days (11.57 days). Children may like to calculate the time in days, hours and minutes. Even 1 000 000 000 (one billion) seconds has passed by the time a person reaches 32 (31.7 yrs). Note: The U.K. now commonly defines a billion as a thousand million (10^9), not a million million (10^{12}).

Counting from one to one million would take longer than $11\frac{1}{2}$ days because as the numbers become larger it would take longer than one second to say each number. Children may also bring up fatigue, losing count and so on as possible difficulties.

See also page 45, A Million Dots and page 47, List of Large Numbers.

A Feel for Big Numbers

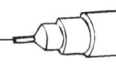

Guideline

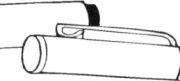

? Did you know that (very strictly speaking) it is easier to become a billionaire in the United States than it is to become a billionaire in the U.K.?

In the United States a billion is 1 000 000 000 but in the United Kingdom and Australia 1 000 000 000 is only a thousand million.

Hints and Ideas

I'm confused. How much money do you need to be called a billionaire in the U.K.?

Find out if you have you lived for a million seconds.

60 minutes in an hour ...
24 hours in a day!
60 seconds in a minute ...

Notes and Calculations

Yes / No

How long would it take to count from one to one million?

Notes and Calculations

Questions

Where will you find the information?

What did you find out?

How will you present your findings?

Findings

www.prim-ed.com – Prim-Ed Publishing

MATHS INVESTIGATIONS

Teacher Background

A Million Dots

The page is included to give students an idea of what a million looks like. The size of a billion starts to come into focus when you realise a thousand of these pages would be required to print 1 000 000 000 dots.

A Million Dots

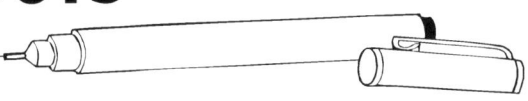

You will need 100 of these pages to make one million dots.

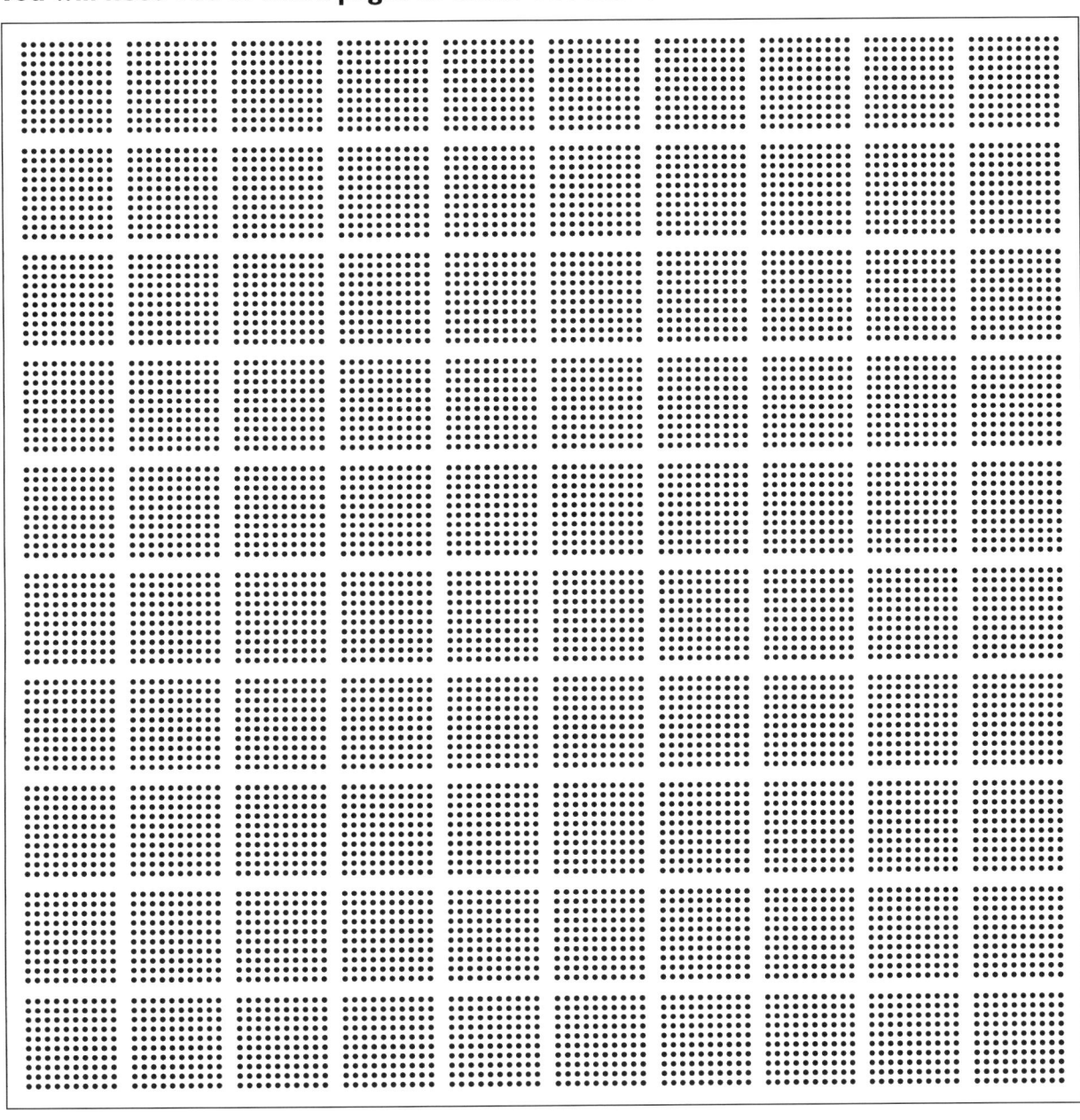

Hints and Ideas

Wow! Do you realise you would need 100 000 of these pages to make a US billion?

I wonder how long it would take if everyone in the school collected a million of the same thing.

How would you organise the counting?

How many pages would it take to make a googol?

I am going to collect one million of something – bread ties, bottle tops, ring pulls from cans …

How much space would it take up?

What's a googol?

100 ×

www.prim-ed.com – Prim-Ed Publishing

MATHS INVESTIGATIONS

Teacher Background

List of Large Numbers

A page containing large numbers is included so students may see the pattern for naming numbers and so the size of numbers written as numerals can be observed. Children may also enjoy the story of how the googol was named. A quick look at the large numbers chart shows that the names occur each time the numbers increase one thousand times or by three zeroes. So, really, a googol is an unusual number in terms of the naming convention.

1×10^{99} – one followed by ninety-nine zeroes is called a duotrigintillion (US) or sexdecilliard (European)

1×10^{102} – one followed by one hundred and two zeroes is called a tretrigintillion (US) or septendecillion (European). The googol fits between these two numbers and does not follow the standard naming convention. A googol is 10 000 000 000 000 000 000 000 000 000 000 000 000 000 000 000 000 000 000 000 000 000 000 000 000 000 000 000 000 000 000 000 000.

The name for this number was made up by a nine-year-old—the nephew of Dr Edward Kasner—an author of mathematics books. He also came up with the name for an even larger number called a googolplex which he described as one followed by as many zeroes as you can write before your hand got tired. A googoplex is one followed by a googol of zeroes or 1×10^{googol}.

Further Investigations

For those interested in large numbers and the American and European naming conventions see

http://www.ecstaticfuturist.com/MiscInfo/numbers.html

David M. Scwartz and Steven Kellog's children's picture book How Much is a Million? (HarperCollins Children's Books, 1985) will provide the stimulus for several investigations. For example, one line reads:

'If you wanted to count from one to one million ... it would take you about 23 days.'

Consider the prefixes used for naming numbers **bi**, **tri**, **quad**, **quin**, **sex** etc.

LIST OF LARGE NUMBERS

American

1	thousand	1×10^3	1 000
1	million	1×10^6	1 000 000
1	billion	1×10^9	1 000 000 000
1	trillion	1×10^{12}	1 000 000 000 000
1	quadrillion	1×10^{15}	1 000 000 000 000 000
1	quintillion	1×10^{18}	1 000 000 000 000 000 000
1	sexillion	1×10^{21}	1 000 000 000 000 000 000 000
1	septillion	1×10^{24}	1 000 000 000 000 000 000 000 000
1	octillion	1×10^{27}	1 000 000 000 000 000 000 000 000 000
1	nonillion	1×10^{30}	1 000 000 000 000 000 000 000 000 000 000
1	decillion	1×10^{33}	1 000 000 000 000 000 000 000 000 000 000 000
1	undecillion	1×10^{36}	1 000 000 000 000 000 000 000 000 000 000 000 000
1	duodecillion	1×10^{39}	1 000 000 000 000 000 000 000 000 000 000 000 000 000
1	tredecillion	1×10^{42}	1 000 000 000 000 000 000 000 000 000 000 000 000 000 000
1	quattrodecillion	1×10^{45}	1 000 000 000 000 000 000 000 000 000 000 000 000 000 000 000
1	quindecillion	1×10^{48}	1 000 000 000 000 000 000 000 000 000 000 000 000 000 000 000 000
1	sexdecillion	1×10^{51}	1 000 000 000 000 000 000 000 000 000 000 000 000 000 000 000 000 000
1	septdecillion	1×10^{54}	1 000 000 000 000 000 000 000 000 000 000 000 000 000 000 000 000 000 000
1	octodecillion	1×10^{57}	1 000 000 000 000 000 000 000 000 000 000 000 000 000 000 000 000 000 000 000
1	novemdecillion	1×10^{60}	1 000 000 000 000 000 000 000 000 000 000 000 000 000 000 000 000 000 000 000 000
1	vigintillion	1×10^{63}	1 000 000 000 000 000 000 000 000 000 000 000 000 000 000 000 000 000 000 000 000 000
Googol		1×10^{100}	10 000 000 000 000 000 000 000 000 000 000 000 000 000 000 000 000 000 000 000 000 000 000 000 000 000 000 000 000 000 000 000 000 000 000

British

1	thousand	1×10^3	1 000
1	million	1×10^6	1 000 000
1	thousand million	1×10^9	1 000 000 000
1	billion	1×10^{12}	1 000 000 000 000
1	thousand billion	1×10^{15}	1 000 000 000 000 000
1	trillion	1×10^{18}	1 000 000 000 000 000 000
1	thousand trillion	1×10^{21}	1 000 000 000 000 000 000 000
1	quadrillion	1×10^{24}	1 000 000 000 000 000 000 000 000

References

Daintith, J & Nelson, R D (Eds) (1989), *The Penguin Dictionary of Mathematics*, Penguin, London

TEACHER BACKGROUND
METRIC PAPER 1

The term 'metric paper' is not really correct. The correct term for the paper we use is the ISO paper size system. The sizes are based on the metric system. Paper may be bought in the A series, such as the common A4 copying paper size, the B series and the C series used for envelopes.

ISO 216 defines the A series of paper sizes as follows:

- The height divided by the width of all formats is the square root of two (1.4142).
- Format A0 has an area of one square metre.
- Format A1 is A0 cut into two equal pieces; i.e.
- A1 is a high as A0 is wide and A1 is half as wide as A0 is high.
- All smaller A series formats are defined in the same way by cutting the next larger format in the series parallel to its shorter side into two equal pieces.
- The standardised height and width of the paper formats is a rounded number of millimetres.

Because all pages conform to the height:width ratio of 1: $\sqrt{2}$ or 1:1.4142, the height and width will never be nicely rounded. An A4 sheet is 297 mm by 210 mm rather than 300 mm by 200 mm.

For a comprehensive explanation of the system see

http://www.cl.cam.ac.uk/~mgk25/iso-paper.html

This system allows for all the various A-size papers to be cut from the larger pieces.

For example, an A3 sheet may be cut to produce two A4 sheets. An A4 sheet may be cut to form two A5 sheets.

A table of A series paper sizes is shown below:

A0	841 × 1 189	1.413
A1	594 × 841	
A2	420 × 594	
A3	297 × 420	
A4	210 × 297	1.414
A5	148 × 210	
A6	105 × 148	
A7	74 × 105	
A8	52 × 74	
A9	37 × 52	
A10	26 × 37	

Most photocopiers provide special keys for enlarging and reducing copies.

A3 → A4	71%	$\sqrt{0.5}$
B4 → A4	84%	$\sqrt{\sqrt{0.5}}$
A4 → B4	119%	$\sqrt{\sqrt{2}}$
B5 → A4		
A4 → A3	141%	$\sqrt{2}$
A5 → A4		

METRIC PAPER 1

Guideline

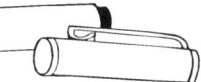

? The piece of paper this activity is printed on is called A4. It measures 297 mm by 210 mm. The next size up is called A3 and is the same size as two A4 sheets joined together. An A5 sheet is half the size of an A4 sheet. The metric paper system ranges from A0 to A10.

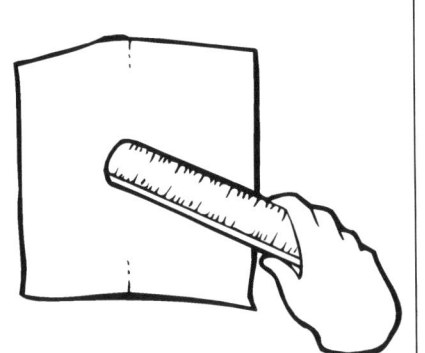

Work our the dimensions of each sheet in the series. How are they related?

Hints and Ideas

Why doesn't an A4 sheet measure 300 mm by 200 mm?

An A0 sheet has an area of 1m². Is it 1 m × 1 m? Why?

I wonder how the enlargement button works on the photocopier.

How many A6 sheets fit into an A3 sheet?

What fraction of an A2 sheet is an A8 sheet?

I pressed 2 √ on my calculator and the number 1.414 ... showed on the display.

I heard that a piece of paper can only be folded seven times.

Notes and Calculations

Questions

Where will you find the information?

What did you find out?

How will you present your findings?

Findings

TEACHER BACKGROUND

METRIC PAPER 2

Encourage children to work in groups, starting with A4 paper to produce an A3, A2, A1 and A0 sheet of paper. This will involve joining the paper with tape. The A0 sheet should have an area close to $1m^2$.

A5 to A10 sheets may then be produced by folding and cutting.

Children can then measure the length and width of each sheet. If the length is divided by the width, the children will see the result is always close to 1.414. You may need to point out that $\sqrt{2} = 1.414$.

Encourage discussion as to why a standard is needed.

Note: when the sheets of paper are laid on the top of each other, a sequence of similar rectangles is formed.

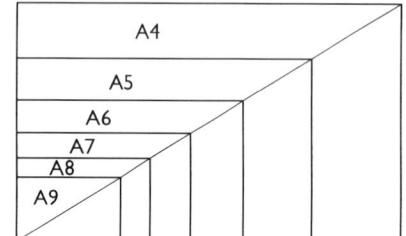

Metric Paper 2

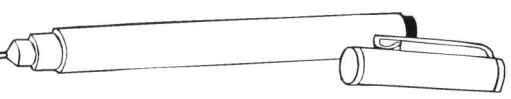

? A selection of paper sizes drawn to scale but not exact size.

What relationships do you notice?

A1 (841 mm x 594 mm)

A2 (594 x 420)

A3 (420 x 297)

A4 (297 x 210)

A5 (210 x 148)

A6 (148 x 105)

A7 (105 x 74)

TEACHER BACKGROUND

PAPER, PAPER EVERYWHERE

When personal computers were first introduced they were accompanied by promises of a paperless office. The reality has been anything but! With many people concerned about the environment, the question of how much paper is used in a typical classroom is of concern. Data is readily available by monitoring classroom use, office and library photocopier use.

Paper is usually sold in **reams of 500 A4 pages. A standard A4 sheet measures 297 mm by 210 mm**. Most reams contain **80 gsm paper**—this stands for **80 grams per square metre**. *Sixteen A4 sheets joined will produce an A0 sheet of paper* which has an area close to one square metre. It is probably easier to weigh a ream of paper and divide by 500 to determine the mass of a single sheet of paper. Given that collecting data of this nature involves making estimates, it is probably simpler to calculate the answer to the nearest ream.

Further Investigations

Stacking several reams on top of one another until the stack is as high as a child will help the class get a feel for larger amounts of paper. Lifting several reams at once will help children appreciate how the mass of paper grows quite quickly. It should also be noted that used paper takes up more space than new, packaged paper.

The price of a ream of paper may be found by examining the price charged at most stationery shops or supermarkets. Children may use this information to determine the cost of paper used.

PAPER PAPER EVERYWHERE

? With the introduction of personal computers, the world was promised a paperless office.

According to the website

http://eetd.lbl.gov/paper/ideas/html/copyfactsM.htm

the typical US office worker uses about 10 000 sheets of copy paper each year.

Work out how much paper your class uses in a week, term and year.

How much paper does your school use in a week? _____

How many reams of paper are bought each year? _____

Hints and Ideas

- How much paper is that? How much would it weigh? How high would it be?
- How much would it cost?
- On the side of a ream of paper it says 80 gsm.
- A ream of paper is made up of 500 sheets.
- What does 'gsm' mean?
- What area is covered by a ream of paper?
- How far would a ream of paper extend if the sheets were joined end to end?
- I wonder how much paper it takes to produce one newspaper.
- How many copies are printed each issue?
- Some papers are thicker than others, especially on the weekend.

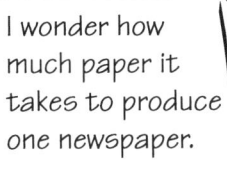

Notes and Calculations

Guideline

Questions

Where will you find the information?

What did you find out?

How will you present your findings?

Findings

TEACHER BACKGROUND

MY LEGS HURT

There are several ways children might tackle this question. For example, they could determine their average pace length and then keep a log of how many paces they walk in a day or a week. Keeping a log for a single day may not be representative of the amount of walking done as the timetable for that day may differ significantly from others.

Children could use a range of measuring devices, such as a **trundle** wheel or a **pedometer**, or they might time how long it takes to move from one class to the next. It is important for the children to come to the realisation that *the purpose of the measurement will determine which measuring tool to use and which units*. For example, knowing it is 20 km from the airport to the city is useful information, but the time taken to drive from the city to the airport is probably more valuable if you are running late to catch a plane!

MY LEGS HURT

Guideline

? In a typical school week children often move around the school to go to different classes; for example, going to the library or the music room.

How far does an individual child travel in a week, term or school year?

Hints and Ideas

How much time is spent moving around a school in a typical week, term, school year?

What is a pedometer?

How far does a teacher travel when on duty?

How would you design a school to reduce the time lost travelling from one room to another?

Notes and Calculations

On a separate sheet of paper, try these challenges.

Challenge

The children in Year 6 are planning to walk in the Lake District as part of a school camp. They plan to walk for two days. How far might they travel?

Hints and Ideas

How far does a person walk in a hour?

How do you think carrying a backpack would affect walking speed?

Do you think a person could keep this pace for 8 hours?

Does a person walk faster going up a hill or on the flat?

Challenge

A 6-year-old boy wandered away from his parents' campsite early one morning. It took four hours to raise the alarm. What search radius would you suggest?

Questions

Where will you find the information?

What did you find out?

How will you present your findings?

Findings

www.prim-ed.com – Prim-Ed Publishing   **MATHS INVESTIGATIONS**

TEACHER BACKGROUND

POPCORN PACKETS

The Popcorn Packets activity is designed to confront the misconceptions that surface area and capacity are linked. This is **not true**—as the popcorn packets demonstrate. It should be noted that *children often confuse volume with capacity*. Capacity may be thought of as the amount a container holds, whereas volume represents the amount of space taken up by an object. For example, a refrigerator has a certain capacity, measured in litres, but takes up a certain amount of space in the kitchen. To add to the confusion, both the words 'volume' and 'capacity' have different meanings outside of the maths classroom; e.g. volume is a button on the TV.

Further Investigations

Another common misconception is that perimeter and area are linked. A good problem to try that exposes this misconception involves fixing the perimeter (e.g. the amount of fencing available) and then altering the dimensions to enclose the largest area.

A farmer has 64 m of chicken wire and wishes to make a chicken yard. How many different-sized yards can be made? Which dimensions produce the yard with the largest area?

POPCORN PACKETS

Guideline

Questions

The Year 6 children at Seatown Primary School are planning to go on school camp. To raise money they decide to sell popcorn at break. The popcorn containers are to be made from a single sheet of A4 paper. The children decided to make cylindrical containers.

Compare the two cylinders that may be made from a sheet of A4 paper. Fill the cylinders with popcorn. You can use other paper to make the bottom of your container. Which popcorn packet will you use when selling popcorn?

Where will you find the information?

Choice _____

Explain the reasons for your choice.

_____
_____
_____
_____

What did you find out?

Hints and Ideas

Both containers must have the same surface area.

How does the capacity compare?

How will you present your findings?

Notes and Calculations

Findings

www.prim-ed.com – Prim-Ed Publishing   57   **MATHS INVESTIGATIONS**

TEACHER BACKGROUND

MEASURE MATTERS I

A horse is measured from the ground to the shoulderblades. The hand measure was originally the width of an adult hand. Today it is the equivalent of four inches or 10.16 cm. Another old measure used in association with horses is the furlong. Originally the furlong referred to a furrow length—the distance that could be ploughed before resting the animal. A furlong is about 200 metres long. Try marking out a distance of 200 metres on the school field. There were exactly eight furlongs to a mile. Most racetracks are basically one-mile ovals and most races are a distance of six furlongs. Along a racetrack you will see poles—each one furlong apart.

The poles are named by their distance from the finish line. For example, the $1/_8$ pole is one furlong from the finish. The $1/_4$ pole is two furlongs ($2/_8$) from the finish. The $3/_4$ pole is six furlongs ($6/_8$) from the finish. This is the point where the gate will be placed for six-furlong races (the most common distance). The poles are colour-coded: $1/_8$ poles are green and white, $1/_4$ poles are red and white, $1/_{16}$ poles are black and white.

Definitions

Some useful background language

Horsepower is the power needed to lift 33 000 pounds a distance of one foot in one minute (about $1\,1/_2$ times the power an average horse can exert). Used for measuring power of steam engines etc.

A **league** is a rather indefinite and varying measure, but usually estimated at three miles (4.83 km) in English-speaking countries.

A **fathom** is six feet (1.83 m), the length of rope a man can extend from open arm to open arm.

The **rope** was lowered into the sea to measure depth.

A **cable length** is the length of a ship's cable, about 600 feet (182.88 m).

One **nautical** mile = 1.1515 miles (1.85 km)

A **knot** is the measure of speed on water. One knot is one nautical mile per hour.

The scattergraph should indicate a strong positive relationship between height and arm span. (See the activity on page 12, Big Foot.)

MEASURE MATTERS I

Horsepower

? While most countries use the SI or metric measurement system, there are still some measurements and expressions we use that relate to the past. For example, horses are measured in 'hands'. Originally, the hand was closed and a measure was taken across its width.

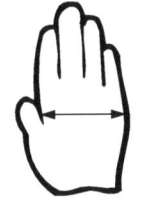

Collect data from your class to produce a class mean hand size.

Mean hand size = _____

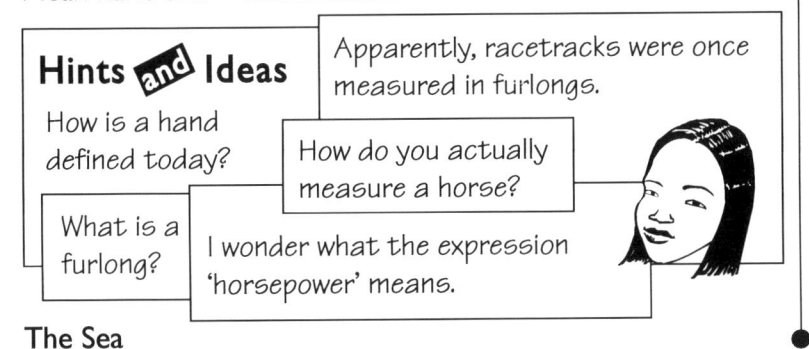

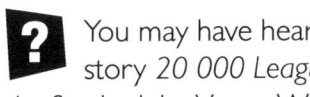

Hints and Ideas
- How is a hand defined today?
- What is a furlong?
- Apparently, racetracks were once measured in furlongs.
- How do you actually measure a horse?
- I wonder what the expression 'horsepower' means.

The Sea

? You may have heard of the story *20 000 Leagues Under the Sea* by Jules Verne. What was a league? There are several other nautical expressions based on old measures. For example, the fathom was used to measure the depth of the sea. A sailor would lower a weighted rope over the side off the ship, wait until it reached the bottom and then haul it in and measure it from the fingertips across his outstretched arms.

On a separate sheet of paper, draw up a scattergraph and plot each child's height and arm span. What do you notice?

Hints and Ideas
- What is a nautical mile?
- What is a knot?

Guideline

Questions

What did you find out?

Findings

Guideline

Questions

How will you collect the information?

Findings

Notes and Calculations

---

www.prim-ed.com – Prim-Ed Publishing   **MATHS INVESTIGATIONS**

TEACHER BACKGROUND

MEASURE MATTERS 2

Some useful background language

span   A span is derived from the distance between the end of the thumb and the end of the little finger when both are outstretched. It is approximately 9 inches or 22.86 cm.

cubit   A cubit is derived from the distance between elbow and tip of the middle finger. It is approximately 18 inches or 45.72 cm.

MEASURE MATTERS 2

Body Measures

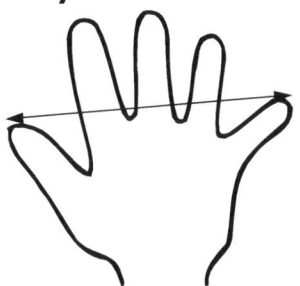

Several old measurement units were based on the body. A span was defined as the distance from the tip of the little finger to the thumb when the fingers were spread.

Collect some data to produce a mean (average) class span.

Mean class span = _____

Our Findings

Builders in ancient Egypt used a measure called a cubit. The cubit was defined as the distance from the elbow to the outstretched middle finger.

Collect data from your class to determine a mean class cubit.

Mean class cubit = _____

I would rather buy my material from a person with a large hand.

Our Findings

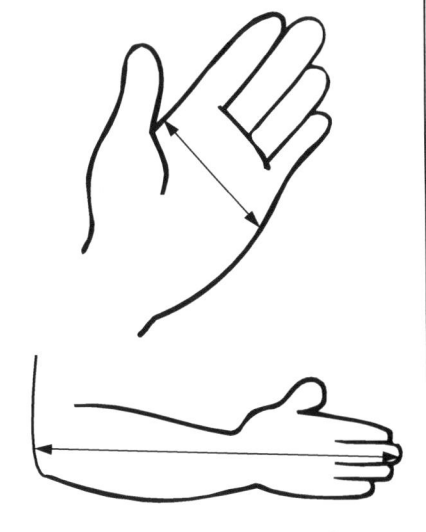

Several other body parts were used to measure. These included the palm—the width across the four fingers of the hand. Another measurement called the hand was based on the distance across all four fingers and the thumb. The finger or digit—the width across the index finger at the first joint—was another measure based on the hand. Choose one of these measures and measure each class member to find who has the longest and shortest length. (Remember to measure to the nearest mm.)

Record your results on a separate sheet of paper.

TEACHER BACKGROUND

MEASURE MATTERS 3

Foot Length

Children may wish to compare their foot length to the distance from their elbow to wrist and note any relationships. In most cases the two lengths will be the same. You could encourage the children to look for other relationships. For example the **length of your thumb matches the length of your nose**. **Twice the distance around your wrist is about the same as the distance around your neck and twice the distance around your neck is about the distance around your waist**. (You may need to be sensitive to any children who are obese when making this comparison.) You may wish to point out that men's shirts are sold according to neck size as the manufacturers realise the relationship between body size and neck size. Many children may also be aware that **arm span and height are roughly the same size**. Children might like to find the record for the tallest person and use paper tape to show his height and armspan

Teaspoons and Tablespoons

In kitchen supply stores you can purchase spoon measures that are calibrated to be used as measuring devices. For example 1/4 teaspoon is 1.25 mL, $^1/_2$ teaspoon is 2.5 mL, 1 teaspoon is 5 mL and a tablespoon is 20 mL. If you look on the side of a medicine bottle, dosages are stated in mL and liquid medicine usually comes with a cup measure. Dosage rates tend to vary by age or weight. Recipes on the other hand simply state, 'add a teaspoon of salt' or a 'tablespoon of honey'. You could ask your students why in the case of medicine the dosage is stated in mL but in recipes teaspoons or tablespoons are used. The issue of heaped teaspoons and flat teaspoons could also be discussed.

Further Investigations

As a result of completing the various activities involving non-uniform measurement techniques, children should develop an understanding of why a common system of measurement was designed. The children may like to investigate the development of the metric system. Many of the terms we use in everyday speech are often related to measurement. Think of all the expressions we use that associated with time; for example, saving time, wasting time and so on. The expression 'in a jiffy', while meaning that you won't be long, has a literal meaning—a 'jiffy' is $^1/_{100}$th of a second.

MEASURE MATTERS 3

? The foot was another body unit used to measure distances. It was defined as the length from the heel to the toe. Complete a table of everyone's foot length.

What do you notice? _____
_____

Why do you think body measures were abandoned in favour of a standard measurement system? _____
_____
_____

While body measures were convenient, people soon realised that the measures varied from person to person and town to town. Even today, when a recipe calls for the use of a tablespoon, the size differs according to the country in which you live.

Several attempts were made to standardise the measurement system. As far back as the 1100s, King Henry I (1100 – 1135) of England decreed that the yard would be the distance from his nose to his thumb when his arm was outstretched.

What was the problem with this standard? _____
_____
_____

In 1215, the king of the time, King John, signed the Magna Carta, which contained numerous laws, including some that pertained to standard measures. Check the Internet or library to see what you can find about measurement systems. A good starting place is:

http://www.ex.ac.uk/cimt/dictinit
http://www.nsc.gov.au

Name	Foot Length

Hints and Ideas

In Britain, a tablespoon might hold 17.7 or 15 mL.

In the USA, a tablespoon only holds 14.2 mL.

In Australia, a tablespoon holds 20 mL. (Big eaters?)

I wonder how much a teaspoon holds.

Our Findings

TEACHER BACKGROUND

MEASURE MATTERS 4

The term used to express normal visual acuity (the clarity or sharpness of vision) is '20/20 vision' and is measured at a distance of 20 feet. If you have 20/20 vision, you can see clearly at 20 feet what should normally be seen at that distance. If you have 20/100 vision, it means that you must be as close as 20 feet to see what a person with normal vision can see at 100 feet.

Having 20/20 vision does not necessarily mean a person has perfect vision—20/20 vision only indicates the sharpness or clarity of vision at a distance.

carat (c)   A measure of the purity of gold, indicating how many parts out of 24 are pure. For example; 18-carat gold is $^3/_4$ pure.

and

200 milligrams or 3.086 grains troy. Originally the weight of a seed of the carob tree in the Mediterranean region. Used for weighing precious stones.

pica $^1/_6$ inch or 12 points

point   .013837 (approximately $^1/_{72}$) inch or $^1/_{12}$ pica. Used in printing for measuring type size.

cricket pitch   Cricket pitch is one chain. A chain was 22 yards (20 m) long and was a measuring instrument used by surveyors.

Yardstick   Yards were an early measuring unit. The size of a yard varied. At one point a yard was defined as the distance from the king's nose to the thumb of his outstretched hand. Eventually most villages had a stick or rod (yardstick) that measured three feet—each of which was 12 inches long—that could be used to check the accuracy of the measurement.

Peck   A peck was a quarter of a bushel. The size of a bushel varied but the English bushel was around 35 L. For simplicity's sake, a peck would be around 9 L.

Further Investigations

For a comprehensive background to the metric system and a history of measurement see The National Standards Commission

http://www.nsc.gov.au

From the website you may download several leaflets.

Leaflet No. 6 contains the 'History of Measurement'.

Leaflet No. 11 contains the 'International System of Units'.

MEASURE MATTERS 4

Guideline

? Even though most countries use the metric system, or the Système International d'Unités—SI for short—there are many words, phrases and measures still in use today that are left over from previous measurement systems. For example, we speak of 'reaching a milestone' as achieving a goal. This expression dates back to Roman times. When the Roman army marched across a country they would set milestones as a measure of distance travelled.

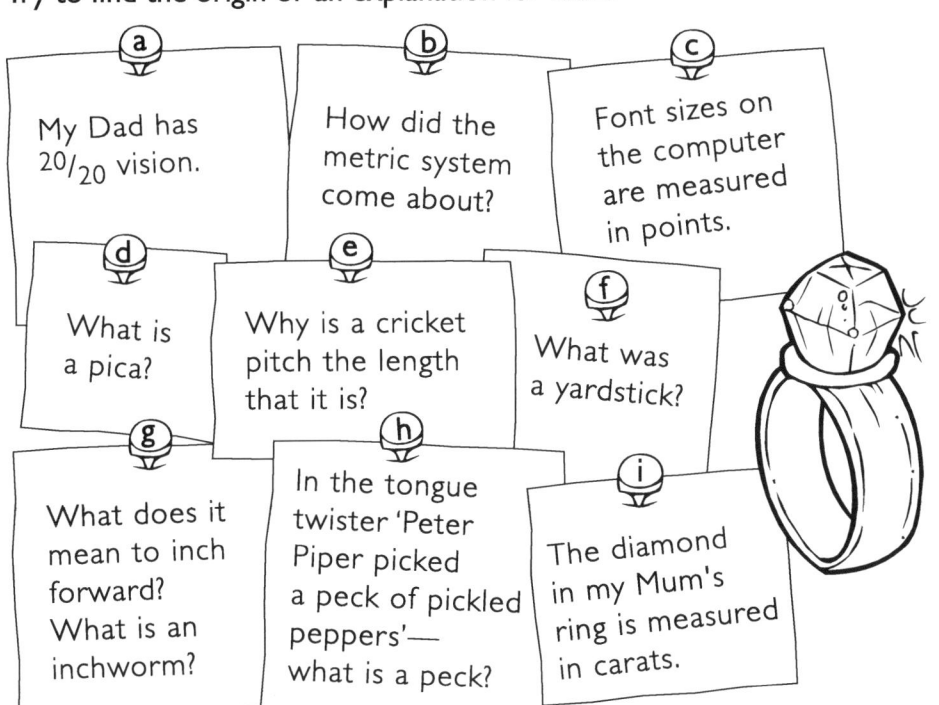

Questions

Several other words and phrases are still used in measurement today. Try to find the origin or an explanation for each.

Where will you find the information?

a My Dad has 20/20 vision.

b How did the metric system come about?

c Font sizes on the computer are measured in points.

d What is a pica?

e Why is a cricket pitch the length that it is?

f What was a yardstick?

What did you find out?

g What does it mean to inch forward? What is an inchworm?

h In the tongue twister 'Peter Piper picked a peck of pickled peppers'—what is a peck?

i The diamond in my Mum's ring is measured in carats.

How will you present your findings?

Hints and Ideas

As the Romans marched they would count out 1 000 paces.

In Roman terms this expression for 1 000 paces was mille passus.

Now I see how the word 'mile' came about!

Notes and Calculations

Findings

www.prim-ed.com – Prim-Ed Publishing

MATHS INVESTIGATIONS

TEACHER BACKGROUND

COIN CAPERS

The Holey Dollar story is a fascinating part of Australian history. You can read about it at

http://www.macquarie.com.au/holey_dollar.htm

Basically, to overcome an acute shortage of money in 1813, Governor Lachlan Macquarie bought silver dollars from Spain and then punched the centres out, thereby producing two coins – the 'holey dollar' (worth five shillings) and the 'dump' (worth one shilling and threepence). Talk about creating money out of nothing—the original silver dollar only cost five shillings! The holey dollar and the dump have been adopted as the symbol for the Macquarie Bank in Australia.

In the U.K., coins are produced at the Royal Mint and banknotes at the Bank of England. For facts about the currency see:

http://www.bankofengland.co.uk

http://www.royalmint.com

The coins stimulus page is designed to encourage children to think about a topic that is often taken for granted—the supply of money. I am sure some children think money grows on trees!

The issue of weighing coins may be used to introduce the topic of coin design—something most people take for granted. Coin design and manufacture is quite complex. The size and weight of the coin need to be considered. For example, if a £1 coin was the same size and weight as a 10p coin but simply a different colour, the makers of vending machines would be up in arms as the machines would have a hard time telling the difference between the two coins.

Once a size and weight are determined, the coin itself must be designed. Who or what will be featured on the coin? The portrait of the current monarch is on one side of all coins. There have been four different portraits of Queen Elizabeth II during her long reign. Since 1970, British historical figures have been depicted on the back of banknotes. The historical figure chosen has to be someone who has made a large contribution to British life.

Further Investigations

The 'life span' of banknotes varies considerably. £5 notes usually last less than one year, whilst £50 notes can last over five years. Why do you think some banknotes last longer than others? Is there a relationship between the value of a banknote and its life span? Each year, one billion new banknotes are printed. Given the life spans of the different banknotes, estimate how many of each banknote are produced.

The Royal Mint presses 600 coins per minute. How many coins are pressed in one hour, a 24-hour day, a 7-day week, a year?

COIN CAPERS

Guideline

Questions

Most people have spare change jingling loose in their pocket or purse. Many children have a moneybox full of coins. We often take our coins for granted, but in the past coins have often been in short supply. For example, when America was just a colony of England, the Americans were not allowed to mint their own coins, so they used a variety of foreign coins, foremost of which was the Spanish milled dollar, or piece of eight, often referred to in pirate stories.

There was a currency shortage in Australia which was solved in 1813 by Governor Lachlan Macquarie. You can read about his ingenious solution to the problem by looking up 'holey dollar' or the 'dump' on the Internet.

How many coins are available in circulation today? Would there be more of some denominations than others?

Where will you find the information?

Explain how you might form an estimate for the number of a particular coin in circulation?

Hints and Ideas

I emptied my moneybox and took £8 worth of 5p coins to the shop to buy sweets and the shopkeeper refused to accept my money. He can't do that, can he?

I took my moneybox to the bank and the bank clerk used a box to separate the coins into various denominations, counted them, bagged them and weighed them!

How does the separator work? Why did the bank clerk weigh the coins? How were the coins bagged?

What did you find out?

How will you present your findings?

Notes and Calculations

Findings

www.prim-ed.com – Prim-Ed Publishing   67   **MATHS INVESTIGATIONS**

TEACHER BACKGROUND

THE LARGEST ORGAN IN YOUR BODY

The answers from using the different approaches will vary and children may wonder about the accuracy of the various methods.

There are several formulas for calculating Body Surface Area, see:

http://www.halls.md/body-surface-area/refs.htm

Each formula or method will produce a slightly different result. For example, two approaches given on the child stimulus page involve using height but not weight. Obviously weight is a factor in determining the surface area of the body.

It is good for the children to see that a range of answers is acceptable and that in the real world a number of different variables affect the calculation.

Further Investigations

There are many allied questions that may be considered when exploring this topic, such as the volume–surface area relationship and why babies dehydrate more quickly than adults. Skin cancer and sunburn are also fruitful areas of discussion. Children might also like to explore what the term 'third-degree burn' means. Is it serious? How many degrees of burn are there?

THE LARGEST ORGAN IN YOUR BODY

Guideline

Questions

? It might surprise you to learn that your skin is the largest organ in your body. Skin protects your body against injury and helps to regulate body temperature. The average adult male has a skin surface area of around 1.8 m² and the average female 1.6 m².

Use newspaper to make a surface area that is either 1.8 m² or 1.6 m².

There are several different ways of calculating your own skin surface area. Try them and compare your results.

- One rough measure involves finding the surface area of your hand and then multiplying by 100.
- Another method involves multiplying the surface area of your foot by 100.
- A third method involves multiplying ³/₅ or 0.6 of your height by your height.
- A fourth method involves doubling your height and then multiplying by the circumference of your thigh.

Where will you find the information?

Hints and Ideas

How many cm² in one m²?
_____

A simple way to count part squares involves only counting squares that are a ½ square or larger.
Forget the rest.

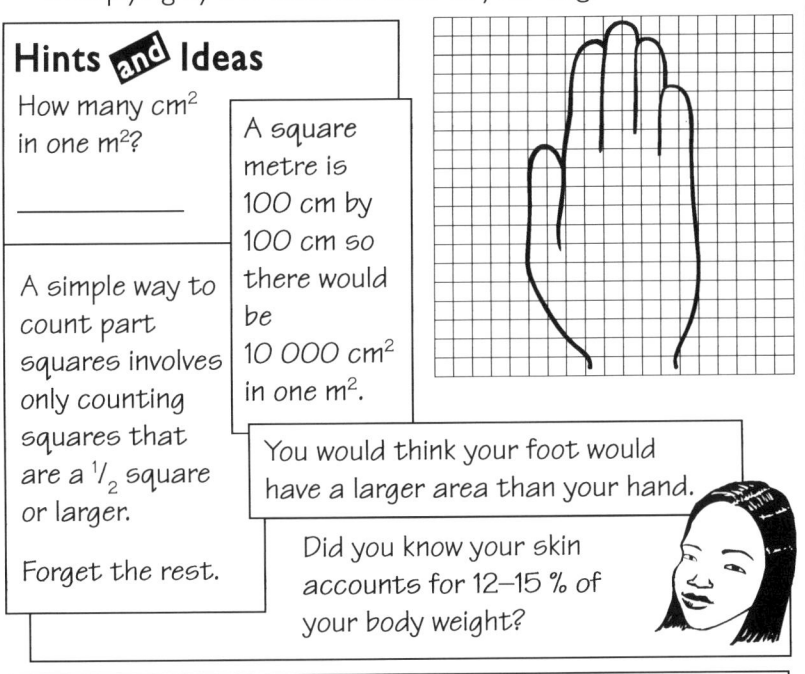

A square metre is 100 cm by 100 cm so there would be 10 000 cm² in one m².

You would think your foot would have a larger area than your hand.

Did you know your skin accounts for 12–15 % of your body weight?

What did you find out?

How will you present your findings?

Findings

Notes and Calculations

Teacher Background

THE LANGUAGE OF MATHS

Many children have trouble with mathematics because of difficulties understanding and interpreting the language associated with the subject. Language dictionaries are commonplace in most classrooms but it is less common to see mathematical dictionaries used in the same way. Encouraging children to explain the everyday mathematical language and terms used in the classroom also helps to uncover any misconceptions children might have.

Further Investigations

A good follow-up activity would involve children searching through newspapers looking for words, expressions and terms related to mathematics. Children could also create posters of associated words when a new topic is developed; e.g. words associated with circles.

THE LANGUAGE OF MATHS

Guideline

Questions

? Have you ever noticed that a lot of unusual words are used in mathematics. This is because a lot of different civilisations have played a role in developing the mathematics we use today.

For example, the word 'decade', which most people apply to a period of ten years, comes from the Greek word deka meaning ten. A decade is literally a group of ten things.

Where will you find the information?

Sometimes a word has several meanings, one in mathematics and others elsewhere. For example, the word 'volume' means the amount of space an object takes up and, also, loudness and softness.

Sometimes we use very specific words rather than general terms. For example, the word 'perimeter' means 'to measure around'. So, we could be asked to find the perimeter of a circle, but generally we are asked to find the circumference of a circle.

What did you find out?

Locate copies of two or three different maths dictionaries and note the way certain words are defined; e.g. square, rectangle, rhombus, polygon, diamond, oblong.

Try making your own 26-word mathematics dictionary containing a word for each letter of the alphabet. Make your definitions simple. You may use diagrams.

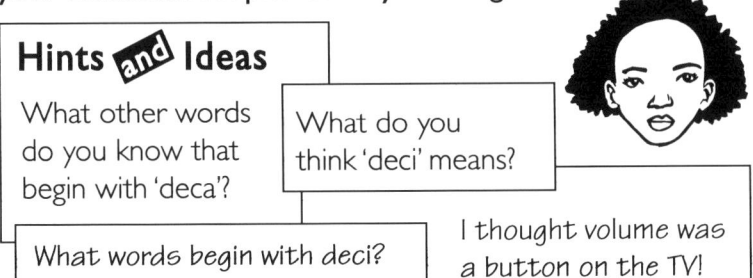

How will you present your findings?

Hints and Ideas

What other words do you know that begin with 'deca'?

What do you think 'deci' means?

What words begin with deci?

I thought volume was a button on the TV!

Findings

Notes and Calculations

www.prim-ed.com – Prim-Ed Publishing   71   **MATHS INVESTIGATIONS**

TEACHER BACKGROUND

PROJECTIONS, ENLARGEMENTS AND DISTORTIONS

Definitions

Dilation: enlarged or reduced

Similar: Same shape but not the same size

Congruent: Same shape and size

This problem is particularly interesting because it illustrates that sometimes a perfect solution to a problem does not exist. It is impossible to represent a sphere (3-D) in two dimensions (map form). The typical map found in most atlases is called a Mercator Projection. This projection misrepresents the relative sizes of land masses so North America, for example, appears much larger than Africa. The area of the continents is given below. (Note: Figures will vary, depending on the reference used.)

Africa: 30 330 000 km^2

Antarctica: 14 250 000 km^2

Asia: 44 444 100 km^2

Australia: 7 682 300 km^2

Europe: 10 531 623 km^2

North America: 24 249 000 km^2

South America: 17 804 526 km^2

The Peters Projection represents the relative sizes of land masses but the shapes of the land masses are distorted. There are several websites that explore this issue in more detail than can be given here.

Children might like to explore the issue of population density by collecting population data for each country. Many social and environmental issues may then be explored.

1	Russia	17 million km^2
2	Canada	9.9 million km^2
3	China	9.6 million km^2
4	United States	9.1 million km^2
5	Brazil	8.5 million km^2
6	Australia	7.6 million km^2
7	India	3 million km^2
8	Argentina	2.7 million km^2
9	Kazakhstan	2.7 million km^2
10	Sudan	2.4 million km^2

Different types of grids are located on pages 75 and 77.

Projections, Enlargements and Distortions

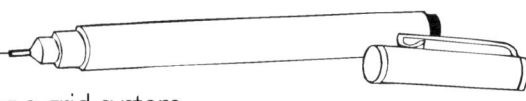

A shape or figure may be dilated, enlarged or reduced using a grid system.

Reduce the figure shown below by copying it onto the 5-mm grid paper.

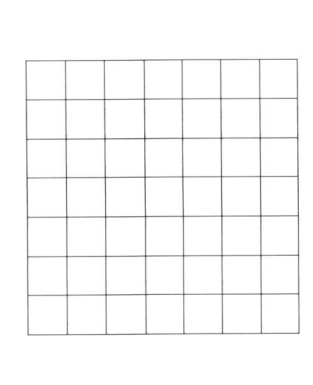

Notice that the reduced figure is similar to the original figure.

Try copying the figure onto the enlarged and stretched grids. (See pages 75–77.) What happens to the figure?

Try using some of the other grids. The result may remind you of the crazy mirror house that you find at shows and carnivals.

Draw your favourite below.

Hints and Ideas

You might be surprised to find that Africa has an area 1.25 times that of North America.

Look at North America and Africa. Which land mass appears to have the largest area?

I wonder why the map looks different.

Take a look at a map of the world and note the size of each of the seven continents.

Try looking on the Internet under Mercator Projection and Peters Projection.

I heard of another map projection called Buckminster Fuller.

www.prim-ed.com – Prim-Ed Publishing   73   **MATHS INVESTIGATIONS**

TEACHER BACKGROUND

PROJECTIONS, ENLARGEMENTS AND DISTORTIONS

To be used with the activity on page 73, Projections, Enlargements and Distortions.

Projections, Enlargements and Distortions

Teacher Background

Projections, Enlargements and Distortions

To be used with the activity on page 73, Projections, Enlargements and Distortions.

Projections, Enlargements and Distortions

TEACHER BACKGROUND

WHO RUBBED THE BLACKBOARD?

Who Rubbed the Blackboard? is an example of taking a standard question (e.g. 15 + 17 = ?) and turning it around (? + ? = 32). By providing children with the answer and asking them to supply the question, a range of possibilities opens up. Rather than restrict the possibilities, children have many different opportunities to show what they know. For example:

15 + 17 = 32 (whole-number solutions)

$14\frac{1}{2} + 17\frac{1}{2} = 32$ (fraction solutions)

14.5 + 17.5 = 32 (decimal solutions)

-5 + 37 = 32 (negative numbers)

Any standard question may be altered this way.

Teaching Point

When children start to mix operations the issue of rule of order will invariably come up. Rather than teach a rule it should be explained that + and − are equally powerful operations and therefore you just complete them from left to right as you work through a calculation; likewise when multiplication and division are included in the same calculation. However, when say addition and multiplication occur in the same calculation, the more powerful operation, multiplication, is done first. Brackets may be used to indicate which part of a calculation should be completed first. Indices such as square (e.g. 4^2) and cube (4^3) are completed before multiplication and division.

WHO RUBBED THE BLACKBOARD?

The teacher walked in as Daniel was cleaning the blackboard. 'Oh no!' she cried. 'I only just finished writing up the questions for the maths lesson.' All that was left showing on the blackboard was the number 32. 'I know,' she said. 'You can come up with some new questions! The only thing is that all the questions you come up with must have an answer of 32.'

Write your questions in the box.

32

Hints and Ideas

I'm going to write multiplication and divison sums.

I'm going to write addition (+) and subtraction (−) sums.

I'm going to write sums that use two operations; e.g. 20 + 20 − 8.

I'm going to include fractions!

What happens if you mix two operations like addition (+) and multiplication (×)?

Notes and Calculations

Teacher Background

The Broken Calculator

(This activity is very similar to 'Who Rubbed the Blackboard'.)

This activity tests the children's ability to work around certain restrictions when performing a calculation. This tests their ingenuity and flexibility with number as well as their knowledge of number properties. Reducing or increasing the number of restrictions revitalises the question. This question may be used to highlight various options. For example:

4 x 8 (use of multiplication/basic number facts)

16 + 16

The answers children provide will give an insight into their understanding of number.

Note: This activity is somewhat contrived as most people who encounter a broken calculator simply throw it away a buy a new one.

The Broken Calculator

? Rachel found a calculator in the bin. Two keys were broken and the display was showing 32. The two broken keys were **3** and **2**. She wondered how the display managed to show 32 when the 3 and 2 keys were broken. She tried various combinations of keys attempting to work out how to get the display to show 32. Try to find as many different ways as possible to make 32 without using the '3' or the '2' buttons.

Write your calculations in the box.

32

Hints and Ideas

I did 100 – 68 to make 32.

I did 8 x 4 to make 32.

Notes and Calculations

WHERE TO FROM HERE?

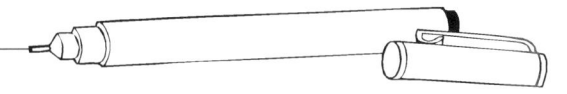

So, you have finished all the open-ended mathematics in the book and the children want more. Where to from here? There are several possibilities.

- Conduct a brainstorming session with the children. Raise 'I wonder' or 'what if' questions.

- Look at the world around you with a mathematical eye.

- Take a rather routine mathematics question and make it messy (see Broken Calculator, Who Rubbed the Blackboard?).

Let me share a few ideas along with a brief explanation of some open-ended mathematics and how it came about. I should explain that I have a family of four boys, including twins, and therefore many of the questions have come about as a result of watching them learn.

- How many hundreds and thousands in a packet?
  This question came about after knocking a packet over.

- How many hundreds and thousands on the top of a fairy cake?

- How many of each colour is there in a M&Ms or Smarties packet?
  My children learnt their colours quickly when they were allowed to eat the sweets afterwards!

  Note: A quick search of the Internet reveals the proportion of each colour in a typical packet. This would lead to some data collection and a number of open-ended questions; but best of all you get to eat the data!

- Design a new toy.
  Just about every family I know has one of those toys you push shapes into.

- What about self-opening doors at supermarkets?

You may also wish to explore Fermi problems. A quick search of the Internet under 'Fermi problems' will provide you with some interesting problems to ponder.